The Best Match

The Best Match
The Soul's Espousal to Christ

Edward Pearse

Edited by
Don Kistler

Soli Deo Gloria Publications
...for instruction in righteousness...

Published by
Soli Deo Gloria Publications
An imprint of Reformation Heritage Books
2965 Leonard St. NE
Grand Rapids, MI 49525
616-977-0889 / Fax 616-285-3246
e-mail: orders@heritagebooks.org
website: www.heritagebooks.org

Reprint 2014

ISBN 978-1-57358-051-9

*For additional Reformed literature, both new and used, request a
free book list from Reformation Heritage Books at the above address.*

Contents

THE BEST MATCH

"I have espoused you to one husband, that I may
present you a chaste virgin unto Christ."
2 Corinthians 11:2

Chapter 1

---

*Wherein an introduction is made into our intended discourse,
the foundation thereof laid, and the matters to be inquired
into in our procedure therein proposed*

A new covenant relation to Christ is certainly a concern of the greatest weight and highest importance to the sons of men of any in the world; it is what lies at the foundation of all true happiness, both in time and eternity. Without it, as a learned divine has well observed, we are not Christians; we are only the carcasses of Christians. Nor may we expect any saving advantage by anything that Christ has done or suffered for poor sinners. And this relation, of so much weight and importance to us, the Scripture represents under various notions and expressions. It is represented to us sometimes under the notion of a king and subjects; hence Christ is called "King of Saints." Sometimes it comes under the notion of a father and his children; hence He is called "the everlasting Father"; and they are His own words unto God the Father: "Behold I, and the children which Thou hast given Me." Sometimes it is represented under the notion of a head and members; hence Christ is said to be the Head of the body, the church; and, on the other hand, believers are said to be the body of Christ and members one of another. And to mention no more, sometimes, as in my text, and frequently elsewhere, it is represented to us under the notion of Husband and wife, Bridegroom and bride, or the soul's espousal to Christ as its own and only Husband. And under this notion I shall, God assisting, speak a little of it, and but a little, no more than to make way for a practical design I have in my eye, which is to woo and allure poor souls into an espousal or marriage covenant with this blessed husband, the Lord Jesus Christ.

That, then, which is before us to be treated of is the marriage or espousal between Christ and believers; and, the better to make way hereunto, you may observe that there is a threefold marriage as relating to Christ and us:

1. There is the personal marriage, and that is between the Person of the Son of God, the second Person in the Trinity, and our nature. This Calvin calls *Verbum Incarnatum,* the Incarnate Word; or, as the evangelist expresses it, "the Word made flesh." This we generally call the hypostatic union.

2. There is the mystical marriage, and that is between the Person of Christ, God-man, and the person of believers, as militant here on earth; the whole Christ and the whole believer being made one. This the apostle calls being joined to the Lord and being one spirit with Him. And this we usually call the spiritual union.

3. There is the heavenly marriage, and that is be-

tween Christ and the Church triumphant above; which, indeed, is the consummation of the two former, and this I would call the glorious union; and what that is I cannot tell, but do hope I am going to see. In the first of these lies the foundation of all our happiness; by the second we are brought into an initial participation of it; by the third we are put into the full possession and enjoyment thereof forever. Now it is neither the first nor the last, but the second of these the apostle here speaks of when he says, "I have espoused you to one Husband, even to Christ"; which accordingly I shall make the subject of my ensuing discourse; which, as also the sum of the apostle's intendment, you may take in this short position: There is a blessed espousal or marriage relation between Christ and believers; or that believers are married or espoused to Christ as their only Husband.

"I have espoused you," says the Apostle, "to one Husband"; not to many but to one, and who is that? Why, Christ, God-man; so the next words declare, "I have espoused you to one Husband, that I may present you as a chaste virgin to Christ." The same is also held forth in other Scriptures. "He that hath the bride is the Bridegroom," said John the Baptist concerning Christ and His Church. And again, "Come hither," says the angel to John, "and I will show thee the bride, the Lamb's wife," that is, the Church, which is the wife and spouse of Christ; but I forbear.

What this espousal or marriage relation between Christ and believers is, as also how it is made up and accomplished, are the principal things to be inquired into for the clearing of what lies before us, which, therefore, I shall address myself unto.

Chapter 2

The espousal or marriage relation between Christ and believers opened, and the import thereof laid down in five things

But what is this espousal or marriage relation between Christ and believers? The Apostle, speaking of it, calls it a great mystery. "This," said he, "is a great mystery; but I speak concerning Christ and His church." I speak of that spiritual marriage that is between Christ and His people, which is indeed a great mystery. It is a hidden, secret thing, a thing hid from human reason and not to be understood but by divine revelation and the light of the Holy Spirit. As far as we apprehend it, you may take this short account in general of it. It is that spiritual conjunction or relation that is between Christ and believers, between the person of Christ and the person of believers, arising from His inhabitation in them by His Spirit and their closing with Him by faith. Much might be said for the opening of this general conclusion, but I shall waive it and give you the true nature of the thing under consideration, more particularly as carrying these five things in it:

1. Free and cordial donation.
2. Near and intimate union.
3. Sweet and lasting communion.
4. Strong and ardent affection
5. Mutual rest and complacency forever.

4

1. *This espousal, or marriage relation, between Christ and believers carries in it a free and cordial donation, a giving of themselves each to other.* In marriages or espousals the parties give themselves to each other; the husband gives himself unto the wife and the wife, by way of return, gives herself unto the husband. They consent to take each other in that relation and, accordingly, to give up themselves each to the other. So, in this spiritual espousal or marriage relation between Christ and His people, there is a giving of themselves each to the other. Christ, on the one hand, gives Himself unto the soul. "I will be yours," says He to the soul, "yours to love you, to save you, to make you happy in Me and with Me. I, with all My riches and treasures, will be fully and forever yours."

"I will be for thee," that is the language of His espousing love unto the soul, Hosea 3:3. And O how sweet is this language! What can Christ give to poor souls like Himself? In giving Himself, He gives the best gift that either heaven or earth affords! In giving Himself, He gives life, He gives peace, He gives grace, He gives righteousness, He gives the favor of God, He gives heaven, He gives all. O sweet gift!

On the other hand, the soul, by way of return, gives himself to Christ. "I will be Thine," says the soul to Christ. "I will be for Thee and not for another." Hence it is said, "They gave themselves to the Lord." They freely and willingly yielded up themselves to Christ to be His, and His forever. "Sweet Jesus, such as I am and have I give to Thee. I am a poor, a sorry gift," says the soul, "infinitely unworthy of Thine acceptance. My best is too bad, my all is too little for Thee; but seeing it is Thy pleasure to call for and accept of such a gift at my hands, I do, with my whole soul, give up myself, my strength, my time, my talents, my all, forever to Thee." And though in truth this is a sorry gift, yet you little think how pleasing, how grateful, it is to Christ, and what a value He puts upon it. You have the whole of this owned and asserted by the spouse, "My Beloved is mine, and I am His."

2. *This espousal or marriage relation between Christ and believers carries in it a near and intimate union.* In marriage, there is a very near union and conjunction between the parties; as they give up themselves each to other, so they become one, each with the other. "They are no more twain, but one flesh." So, in this espousal or marriage relation between Christ and believers, there is a very near union and conjunction between them. The two are made one, and thus the apostle sets forth the marriage between Christ and them, "For this cause shall a man leave father and mother, and shall be joined unto his wife, and they two shall be one flesh. This is a great mystery; but I speak concerning Christ and the church," that is, I speak of the marriage relation which is between Christ and the church, and which consists in union. Hence also believers are said to be joined to the Lord and to be one spirit with Him. So that espousing to Christ and being joined to Christ are all one.

The truth is, herein lies the very soul and substance of this spiritual marriage, in a spiritual union between Christ and the believer. Though Christ and the soul were two before, two who were strangers to each other, yet in this marriage or espousal they become one, and so much one that all the world can never make them two again, can never dissolve this union. By this usual, but of all others most pleasant, metaphor of a bridegroom and bride is expressed and set forth the spiritual union that is between Christ and the church, Christ and every holy soul. And this union is a full union, a union between the whole person of Christ and the whole person of the believer; the whole person of Christ is united unto the believer and the whole person of the believer is united unto Christ. Neither is our soul alone joined with the soul of Christ alone; nor is our flesh alone joined with the flesh of Christ alone; but the whole person of every believer is truly joined with the whole person of Christ.

On the one hand, the whole person of Christ is united to the believer. The believer's union with Christ is neither with the divine or human nature considered apart, but it is with the whole person consisting of both natures. And, indeed, else they could not be said to be united to Christ; for neither of the natures, considered apart, is Christ. We cannot say that the divine nature is Christ, or that the human nature is Christ; but Christ is both the divine and human nature, God-man, in one Person. Christ is not a name of either nature, but of the Person consisting of both natures, together with His office. Besides, were we united only to one nature, and not to the whole person of Christ, what would our union avail us? Surely it would be vain and ineffectual; for Christ Himself tells us that "it is the Spirit which quickeneth, the flesh profiteth nothing"; that is, the flesh or human nature of Christ considered alone and without the influence of the divine avails nothing to souls as to their spiritual or eternal good. Nor indeed can the human nature of Christ, without the divine, give grace or any spiritual good thing.

On the other hand, were we united to the divine nature alone, and not to the human, then our union would be as ineffectual; for however full the divine nature is of grace and life in itself, yet nothing can thence be derived and communicated to us but by and through the humanity. And, indeed, as the humanity profits nothing without the divinity, so, I may say, the divinity will profit us nothing without the humanity. Hence it is that Christ so often speaks of "eating His flesh and drinking His blood," and withal asserts the necessity thereof in order to life and happiness by Him. What does eating His flesh and drinking His blood signify but a union with His humanity? And, therefore, He adds, "He that eateth my flesh, and drinketh my blood, dwelleth in Me, and I in Him," which is an expression of union; and without this we have, we can have, no life, no grace from Him.

In a word, as the humanity has nothing to give or communicate to us, no life, no grace, no spiritual blessing without the divinity, so the divinity is incommunicable to us without the humanity. And, therefore, were our union with the one only, without the other, it must be ineffectual. I will close this with the saying of an eminent divine, "Although all life, all salvation, flows from the fulness of the Deity that is in Christ, yet, notwithstanding, it is not communicated to us but *in* the flesh, and *by* the flesh of Christ. For the Deity is as the fountain whence all good things flow, life and salvation; but the flesh, or humanity, is the channel by which all these good things, and all gifts and graces, are derived unto us. Therefore, unless a man apprehends this channel and is united to it he cannot possibly be made a partaker of these waters which flow from this fountain."

On the other hand, the whole person of the believer is united to Christ; not his soul only without his body, nor yet his body only without his soul, but his whole person, consisting of both soul and body in conjunction. As Christ is the Savior, so He is the Head of the whole person of every believer; for He saves none but those whom He is Head unto. And as Christ is the Head of, so He must have union with, the whole person of every believer; for His being a Head implies union, and that union must extend as far as His headship does, even to the whole person. In short, the believer's soul is united to Christ. Therefore, said the apostle, "He that is joined to the Lord is one spirit; and the believer's body is united to Christ, and therefore the bodies of believers are said to be members of Christ." Thus this union is a full union; and, as it is a full, so it is a very near union. Next to those two great unions, the essential union, the union of the three Persons in one and the same Divine Essence, and the personal union, the union of the two natures, divine and human, in the Person of Christ, is the nearest union. Hence it is expressed sometimes by their being in each other. "He that eateth My flesh and drinketh My blood, dwelleth in Me and I in you." And what can be nearer than to be and dwell in each other? It is a nearer union than that between the husband and the wife, for that union may be broken, and is at last; but this never is, never can be broken, as in its place will be shown.

3. *This espousal or marriage relation between Christ and believers carries in it full and lasting communion.* In a marriage relation there is a full and free communion between the parties, both in what they are and what they have. The husband admits the wife into a participation in all he is and has. On the other hand, he communicates with her in all she is and has; and, indeed, union is in order to communion. So it is here in the espousal or marriage relation between Christ and believers: there is a full and free communion between them in all they are and have. On the one hand, Christ communicates Himself unto the believer; He admits him into a fellowship and participation with Him in all His riches and fulness. Hence "of His fulness have we all received, and that grace for grace." He is said to be "full of grace," and what grace is that? Why, all graces, personal grace, purchased grace, grace of privilege, and grace of influence. And here it is said, that of His fulness have we all received; not some only, but all, great and small, have received, and that not in a low, poor, scanty measure only but in great abundance. Therefore, it is added "and grace for grace," or grace upon grace, heaps of grace, grace in a plentiful manner, all grace needful for the soul—righteousness, remission of sins, sanctification, renovation of the spirit, and the like. Behold, whatever Christ is or has, which believers are capable of, is all theirs, and they all hold communion with Him therein. His beauty is theirs; and however black and deformed they are in themselves, yet they are fair and comely in Him. Hence said the spouse, "I am black, but comely," that is, black in myself but comely in Christ; black by nature but comely by the Redeemer's grace. I am comely through the

comeliness which He puts upon me.

His righteousness is theirs, and, however guilty and unrighteous they are in themselves, yet in Him they are righteous and stand perfectly righteous in the sight of God. Hence His name is said to be "The Lord our Righteousness," and they are said to be made "the righteousness of God in Him." His privileges and dignities are theirs; and however vile and base they are in themselves, yet in Him they are highly dignified and advanced.

Is He a Son? So are they through Him. "To as many as received Him, to them gave He power to become the sons of God, to as many as believed in His name."

Is He an Heir, an Heir of God? So are they; they are heirs, yea, "co-heirs with Him of God."

Is He beloved by the Father, and that with a choice and singular love? So are they; they are beloved in Him; yea, they are beloved with the same love wherewith He is beloved by the Father.

Is He a King? So are they. He has made them, and makes them all kings, and they do and shall reign with Him forever and ever.

Is He in heaven, in possession of happiness and glory? So are they; hence they are said to "sit together with Him in heavenly places."

What shall I say? His glory is theirs. "The glory which Thou gavest Me (said He to His Father) I have given them." Yea, all His divine fulness is theirs, and however empty and imperfect they are in themselves, yet they are "perfect and complete in Him," and in His fulness. "In Him dwelleth all the fulness of the Godhead bodily"; bodily, that is, truly, perfectly, unchangeably; and not typically only, as in the temple of old. All the fulness and perfection of the Godhead dwells truly and perfectly in Him. And what then? Why, it follows, "and ye are complete in Him." You are poor and empty things in yourselves, but your Head and Husband has all the fulness of the Godhead in Him, and it is always in Him, for it dwells in Him. And it is all yours, and you communicate with Him in all, as far as you are capable of it, to complete you both in grace and glory. Thus Christ communicates Himself unto the believer and admits him into a participation with Him in all He is and has.

On the other hand, Christ partakes and holds communion with believers in all they are and have. And what is their all? Truly a poor all; in and of themselves they have nothing but sins and sorrows, guilt and affliction. Indeed, in marrying them, He gives them gifts, graces, comforts, and the like; and, having given them these, He holds communion with them in all. Their gifts and graces, their joys and comforts are His; but, I say, in and of themselves they have nothing but sorrows and sins, and He, in a sort, holds communion with them in both. Hence it is said, "in all their afflictions He is afflicted."

He looks upon their sorrows as His and their sufferings as His. "I was hungry, and ye gave Me no meat; I was thirsty, naked, imprisoned." And often, you know, in Scripture their sufferings and afflictions are called the sufferings and afflictions of Christ; and why the sufferings and afflictions of Christ? Not only because, for the most part, they suffer for His sake, but also because He suffers and is afflicted in them and with them. He communicates with them in their afflictions, and, as in their sorrows, so also in some sort in their sins, too.

Hence He calls their sins His as well as their afflictions.
"Mine iniquities have taken hold upon me," Psalm
40:12. Luther and others understand this to be Christ
speaking of our sins and calling them His; not, my
beloved, that He admits of any the least stain or tincture of sinful defilement upon Himself, but He so
looks upon our sins as His as to take them off from us,
and looks upon Himself responsible to the Father's
justice for them. So He was said to be "made sin for
us." O what grace is here! I close this head with a great
and sweet saying which I have read in one of the ancients, suitable to this purpose: "The like sweet names
are not to be found, by which the sweet affections of
Christ and the soul are expressed each to other, as
those of the bridegroom and bride; for why, all things
are common with them; nothing proper, having nothing separate and apart each from other; they have both
one inheritance, one house, one table, one marriage
bed, also one flesh. The sum is, they communicate with
each other in all they are and have."

4. *This espousal or marriage relation between Christ and
believers carries in it strong and ardent affections.* In the
marriage relation, there is the dearest, strongest, and
most intimate affection that is to be found among the
children of men. It is a relation made up of love. Love
is not only a concomitant of marriage but it is even a
part of it, and is essential to it. In marriage, hearts must
be joined as well as hands, or they are not right. So
here, in this spiritual espousal or marriage relation between Christ and believers, there is a very dear and
very intimate affection each to other. Their hearts are
indeed knit, and intimately cleave to one another.

"The saints," says one, "are called the spouse of Christ, because of that great and unparalleled love that is between them." And it is a sweet saying which I have read in one of the ancients to this purpose, "Christ calls Himself our Bridegroom that He might insinuate the greatness of His love to us, which decays not with time; and He calls us His spouse, not His wife, noting that our love to Him should be always new, always lively and vigorous."

The truth is, there is no love like that between Christ and His spouse. Christ loves and espouses, and the soul loves and is espoused; and both, being espoused, love forever. And so this relation is both founded in love and perfected in love; it is both made up and managed with love on all hands. Christ sets His love upon the soul and, in that love, espouses him to Himself; and having, in this love of His, espoused him to Himself, then He loves him as His spouse.

Often in Song of Solomon His spouse is called His love; as also He, on the other hand, is called her Beloved. And what does this note but that the whole relation consists mainly in love, and that they are more dearly and intimately beloved by each other? Christ having espoused the soul to Himself, now His love runs out in full streams towards him. He loves him above all the rest of the creatures, in some respects above the angels themselves, as standing in a nearer relation to Him than they do. On the other hand, the soul's love is drawn out to Christ and, loving Him, is espoused to Him; and, being espoused to Him, he loves Him yet more. Now Christ "is laid between his breasts," in his most intimate affections He has the throne in his heart; yea, the soul by degrees comes to be "sick of

love" to Him, as you have it, Song of Solomon 2:5.
"Stay me with flagons," says she. "Comfort me with apples, for I am sick of love." To whom? To Christ. "And
truly this," as one of the ancients has observed, "is a
sweet sickness, a blessed languor, a pleasant love." And
this love between Christ and His spouse is a chaste
love, a virgin love, a love that is pitched upon the person of each other. Christ loves the person of the believer and the believer loves the person of Christ. Of
which more in its place.

5. *This espousal or marriage relation between Christ and
believers carries in it a mutual rest and complacency forever.*
In a marriage relation there is great delight and complacency the parties have, or should have, in each
other, especially in the day of espousals. You know how
Solomon spoke, "Rejoice with the wife of thy youth, let
her be as the loving hind and pleasant roe: let her
breasts satisfy thee at all times, and be thou ravished
always with her love." All this notes that joy, rest, and
complacency that this relation carries in it, and the
parties have in each other. We read (you know) of the
joy of the bridegroom as the highest and purest that is
found among the sons of men. So, in this spiritual espousal between Christ and believers, there is a mutual
rest and complacency which they have in each other.
They are, as it were, the rest, the joy, the satisfaction of
each other, the solace of each other's souls.

On the one hand, Christ rests and rejoices in the
believer, as one would do in the wife of his youth. Thus
His spouse is to Him "as a loving hind and a pleasant
roe," and He lives joyfully with her. Hence she is His
delight, and that as being married to Him: "Thou shalt

be called Hephzibah," says He to her, "for the Lord delighteth in thee"; you shall be the joy and delight of My
soul. And again, "As a young man marrieth a virgin, so
shall thy sons marry thee; and as the Bridegroom re-
joiceth over the Bride, so shall thy God rejoice over
thee." The sum of all which amounts to this: that
Christ, marrying His people to Himself, delights in
them, and rejoices over them, and that with the highest and purest delight and complacency of all others, a
delight and complacency suitable to the relation. The
truth is, He speaks as if all His delight were in them, as
if He had forgotten to delight in the angels, or in any
of the works of His hands, but in them alone. "My
goodness," says He to the Father, "does not extend to
Thee, but to the saints, in whom is all my delight."

Yea, He declares Himself ravished with them as His
spouse, "Thou hast ravished my heart, my sister, my
spouse; thou hast ravished my heart"; and He speaks as
one ravished indeed. "How fair and pleasant art thou,
O love, for delight!" He acknowledges Himself capti-
vated by her: "Turn away thine eyes from Me, for they
have overcome me." Yea, He has declared them to be
His rest: "This is My rest forever," says He, "here will I
dwell, for I have desired it." It is spoken of Zion as a
type of the church and spouse of Christ and His rest in
her. And indeed they are His rest. His soul is at rest in
them. In them is His highest joy. Hence that sweet
word, Zephaniah 3:17, "The Lord thy God in the midst
of thee is mighty; He will save, He will rejoice over thee
with joy; He will rest in His love upon thee, He will joy
over thee with singing"; as much as to say, "His whole
rest, solace, and delight shall be in you."

On the other hand, the believer rests and rejoices

in Christ as in his Head and Husband. "I sat down under His shadow," says the spouse, "with great delight." She did, as one expresses it, sweetly rest and repose her soul in Him. Her soul was at rest and filled with delight, great delight; she had great springing of joy within her, and all this in Christ her bridegroom; in His person, in His presence, in His protection, in the fruits of His grace and love. And, therefore, it follows, "and His fruit was sweet to my taste"; as if she would say, "O with what joy, what solace, what delight and satisfaction of soul did I converse with Him, and feed upon Him!"

Thus, in these espousals there is mutual delight and satisfaction between Christ and believers; and O how sweet is this! This makes this espousal to relish so strongly of heaven, and to set the soul down even at the gate thereof. Thus I have shown you what this espousal or marriage relation between Christ and believers is.

Chapter 3

In which the way and means of the accomplishment of this espousal or marriage relation between Christ and believers is enquired into, and a general account thereof given

Having seen something of the nature of the espousal or marriage relation between Christ and believers, the next thing to be enquired into is how this espousal or relation is made up and accomplished. To be sure, naturally we are all strangers to it and unacquainted with it, being, as the apostle speaks, "without Christ," that is, without union with Him or any spiritual relation to Him. But how, then, and in what way is it brought about? In general, it is from divine grace, the grace of God in Jesus Christ acting and laying out itself for us and upon us. And it is from divine grace two ways, or as that grace carries a double opposition with it. First, as it stands in opposition to any thing of worth or deservings in us; and so it flows from the riches of divine grace as its only spring and fountain. Second, as that grace stands in opposition to anything of power or ability in us; and so it is affected by the power of divine grace as its principle and efficient cause. Accordingly, take this in these two propositions:

1. *This espousal or marriage relation between Christ and believers flows from the riches of divine grace as its only spring and fountain.* That any of the sons of men are married

18

and espoused to Christ is not from anything of worth
or deservings in them, but purely and entirely from
free grace and love dwelling and working in the heart
of God and Christ towards them. And this account the
Scripture gives us of it in Jeremiah 31:3, "I have loved
thee with an everlasting love, therefore with lovingkindness have I drawn thee." As if He should say, "I
have drawn you out of your sins, out of your unbelief,
out of your carnal rests and refuges. And I have drawn
you to Myself, into a union, a communion with Myself;
into a marriage-covenant and relation with Myself. And
all this from My own free love, that love, that kindness,
that has been in My heart towards you from everlasting." So again, Hosea 2:19, "I will betroth thee unto Me
forever; yea, I will betroth thee unto Me in righteousness, and in judgment, and in loving kindness, and in
mercies." Mark, it is mercy and lovingkindness which
espouses souls to Christ. "God," says one upon this
place, "espouses us to Christ, induced thereunto by no
merits of ours but by His own goodness and mercy."

And indeed, my beloved, what have we, or what
have any of the sons of men, that should speak the one
or the other worthy of a conjugal relation to Christ, or
that should invite and induce Him to take us into such
a relation to Himself? Have we birth or parentage to
induce Him? No, alas! As to our state, we are all of the
brood of hell, and thence, as sinners, we have all our
descent and origin, John 8:44. Have we beauty and
amiableness? No, for we are all black and deformed in
ourselves. We have the spirit of the devil in us and the
image of the devil upon us. We are blind, deaf, dumb,
lame, and crooked. So the Scripture speaks of us in
our natural state. We are all in our blood and gore,

cast out into the open fields to the loathing of our persons, Ezekiel 16:5-6. And as their case is represented, Isaiah 16, such is ours spiritually: even from the sole of the foot to the crown of the head there is no soundness in us, nothing but wounds and bruises and putrefying sores. In a word, we are all sin and have nothing but sin. Know, O spouse of Christ, you have nothing of yourself but sins. As for all your good things, they are the grace of your Bridegroom to you, to whom, therefore, give the glory of it.

I say, we have nothing but sin. And is there any beauty, any comeliness, in that to attract a holy Jesus? Surely not. Have we riches and treasures? No, for indeed we are "poor and miserable and blind and naked." Treasures it is true we have, but they are black ones—treasures of sin and wickedness, treasures of guilt and wrath—which surely cannot render us worthy, but most unworthy of such a relation. Have we wisdom and parts to invite Him? No, we are altogether brutish and foolish. Wise we are, but it is to do evil. To do good we have no knowledge. Have we love and kindness in us towards Him, good nature? No, for naturally we love Him not; yea, we hate Him and are enemies to Him. We hate both Him and the Father, as He charged the Jews of old. Yea, we are as enmity itself to Him. We are enemies to His person, to His kingdom, to His grace, to His righteousness, to His ways, and to all acquaintance and communion with Him. Thus, we have nothing to induce Him to take us into such a relation. At best we are but poor worms whose foundation is in the dust. And what can it be but free and rich grace in Christ to marry and espouse such unto Himself?

2. *This espousal or marriage relation between Christ and believers is wrought and effected by the power of divine grace as its principle and efficient cause.* When souls are married and espoused to Christ, it is not done by any power or ability of their own, nor yet by the power and efficacy of means and instruments, but it is purely from the power and efficacy of divine grace. Indeed, God makes use of means and instruments. He makes use of the gospel and gospel ministers for the espousing of sinners to His Son. And these are the only ordinary ways and means whereby He does it. Therefore, says the Apostle in my text, "I have espoused you to one husband." That is, by my ministry, by preaching the everlasting gospel, I have been an instrument in God's hand for your espousing to Christ.

But though God thus makes use of means and instruments in this work, yet still the work itself is from pure grace, and to grace Christ attributes it, excluding all other power but this as sufficient hereunto. "No man can come to Me," or believe on Me, close with Me in a marriage covenant, "except the Father which hath sent Me draw him"; that is, except the power of divine grace is put forth upon him in order hereunto. The drawing Christ speaks of here is comprehensive of the whole business; 'tis the enabling of us to come to Christ, to believe on Him, and to close with Him as our Head and Husband. It notes (as one observes) not any violent co-action or constraint, but a sweet bowing of the will which in itself was averse from and opposite to God and Christ and, withal, carrying the soul to Christ and enabling him to close with Him in this relation. And this Christ ascribes wholly to the power of divine grace. The truth is, in and of ourselves we have no power or ability for such a work, we are "without strength." Yea, when we are brought into Christ by the power of divine grace, yet then, in and of ourselves, we can do nothing; so Christ tells us, "without Me ye can do nothing." Yea, when we are brought into Christ, and have had some communion with Him, yet we can't follow after Him nor draw one tittle nearer to Him unless a fresh influence of divine grace is put forth upon us, enabling us thereunto.

So much the spouse was sensible of and, therefore, prays thus, "draw me and we will run after Thee." As if she should say "Lord, in myself I can't stir one foot towards Thee, but put forth Thy power in drawing me, and then, and not till then, shall I come nearer to Thee."

Yea, my beloved, the espousing of souls to Christ is not only the act or work of divine grace, and the power of it, but 'tis the act or work of the mighty power of that grace. 'Tis not an ordinary power that is and must be put forth therein but even the greatness of the power of that grace, a power no less than that which was put forth in raising Christ from the dead. So the Apostle tells us, "That ye may know what is the exceeding greatness of His power to usward who believe, according to the working of His mighty power which He wrought in Christ when He raised Him from the dead." So then, here is the mighty power of God, the greatness of the mighty power of God, the exceeding greatness of the mighty power of God, the same exceeding greatness of the mighty power of God which raised Christ from the dead, and all put forth to enable us to believe and so to close with Christ in a marriage covenant. Thus, this work is every way from divine grace. But here, more particularly, the enquiry will be what those acts or works of divine grace are by which poor sinners come to be espoused to Christ. I shall reduce them all to two heads. First, more remote, being acts of divine grace put forth for us and towards us; or, secondly, more near, being acts of divine grace put forth in us, and upon us. In the first, the Father and Jesus Christ work more immediately by and from themselves. In the second, they work by the influence and ministry of the blessed Spirit. I'll speak a little of each.

Chapter 4

Wherein are contained the more remote acts of divine grace, put forth more immediately by the Father and Jesus Christ, for us, and towards us, in order to the accomplishment of the espousal between Christ and us

There are some more remote acts of grace, acts of grace put forth more immediately by the Father and Jesus Christ, for us, and towards us, in order to the making up of this espousal or marriage relation between Christ and us, and of these I shall mention five, all which do necessarily concur and have their influence into this business, and indeed there is much of the mystery of God in them. They are these:

1. *God the Father marries and espouses our nature to the Person of His Son and thereby fits and prepares Him to be a Husband for us.* This God has done once for all, and the influence thereof concurs unto the accomplishment of the espousal between Christ and every believer. I shall illustrate this unto you from that parable where we read of a king that made a marriage for his son, by which king we are to understand God the Father, and, by His Son, Jesus Christ, the eternal Son of that eternal Father, He who proceeded from Him by eternal generation. God the Father, then, is said to make a marriage for His Son; but pray, who is the spouse? 'Tis observed by divines that the spouse is not here mentioned. Who or what, then, is she? 'Tis answered,

Christ has a twofold spouse, our nature and the persons of believers, both which may be intended here, though the first chiefly and principally. And so, by the marriage here we are to understand the personal marriage, the marriage between the person of the Son of God and our nature; and so Calvin and others expound it. This is the primary significance, but secondarily and, by consequence, the spiritual marriage between Christ and believers. And we are to look on the one as the laying a foundation and making way for the other; so that the whole resolves into this, that God the Father has married and espoused our nature to the Person of His Son in the hypostatic union and, thereby, has fitted and prepared Him to be a Husband for us, and made way for the marriage of our persons to His Person in the spiritual union.

And, indeed, unless our nature had been first married to Him in the one, our persons could never possibly have been married to Him in the other; for, pray observe, the glory of Christ considered as the eternal Son, and so as God, is too bright, and the distance between Him and us is too great for us to come to Him, and be made one with Him in a marriage relation. Christ considered in His own naked glory as God is too bright an object for us to look upon, much more to have so near a union to, and communion with. One sight of Him thus considered is enough to swallow us up, and even to overwhelm our spirits. We cannot thus see Him and live; but now, our nature being married and espoused to His divine Person, that is to say, He having assumed our nature into union with Himself as the eternal Son, which the evangelist calls His being made flesh, John 1:14, and the Apostle calls it His partaking of flesh and blood, Hebrews 2:14, hereby the overwhelming brightness of His glory is veiled and the dreadful terror of His greatness, together with the frightening distance between Him and us, is taken away. Yea, hereby His glory is brought down (as one has it) to our eye, to our beholding. Hereby He has marvellously sweetened and endeared Himself to us, and made way for us for a free access to Him and the nearest union and communion with Him.

Hence divines give us this as one reason of Christ's incarnation, that He might thereby become a fit Husband for His people, and they might be capable of union and communion with Him. Therefore (as a learned man has observed) was the Son of God made man, that He might be a true, a fit Bridegroom for the church; and 'tis rightly observed by divines that, in strict propriety of speech, neither the Father, nor the Holy Spirit, but the Son, the second Person in the Trinity, is the Church's Bridegroom; and they give this reason for it: because He only was made man; He only was incarnate. O, had not the Son of God been incarnate, had He not (as Austin's expression is) married our nature to Himself in the womb of the virgin, none of us would ever have been capable of such a privilege, such a happiness, as a conjugal union and communion with Him. That, therefore, is the first act of grace in this business.

2. *God the Father gives Christ unto the soul and the soul to Christ. He gives Christ for a Head and Husband to the soul, and He gives the soul for a bride or spouse to Christ.*

First, He gives Christ for a Head and Husband to the soul. In John 4:10, Christ is called "the gift of God," and how is He the gift of God? In two ways: First, in that He gave Him for us, and gave Him to be incarnate—to suffer, to bleed, to die, to be made sin and a curse for us. He gave Him as an offering and a sacrifice for us. And, second, in that He gives Him also to us. He gives Him to be a Head and Husband. Hence it is said that He gave Him to be "Head to the church," and such a Head as has the command and disposal of all things. "He gave Him to be Head over all things to the Church," both in the counsel of His will from eternity, and also in the work of His grace here in time. He thus gives Christ to us, and O how richly and gloriously does His grace shine forth herein! In giving Christ to us He gives His best and His dearest. For He has nothing better, nothing dearer to Him, than His Christ, as afterwards may be shown.

Second, He gives the soul for a bride or spouse to Christ. Believers are often said to be given by the Father to Jesus Christ. "My Father who gave them to Me," says Christ concerning believers, "is greater than all." And "Thine they were, and Thou gavest them to Me," with many other places which might be mentioned. God gives all the elect to Christ to be His spouse. He gives them to Him, first, in the eternal purpose and counsel of His grace. In the day of everlasting love, when God first set His heart upon His chosen ones, then gave He them to His Son and willed their union to Him in a marriage covenant. And He gives them to Him, second, in the work of vocation, which makes way for the working of faith in Christ in the soul. The Father, says he, has given this spouse to His Son (speaking of His Church), and joins her to Him by His Spirit. And, my beloved, without this act of grace put forth by God towards us, the match would never be made between Christ and any poor soul. For this indeed is that which brings the soul to Christ. So much Christ Himself tells us, "All that the Father giveth Me shall come to Me." Mark, it is the Father's giving us to Christ that brings us to Him, and were we not by the Father given to Him we should never come to Him by believing. There could never be a marriage relation between Him and us.

3. *Christ readily approves and accepts the Father's gift, being willing, yea, longingly desirous, to espouse them unto Himself whom His Father gives Him in order thereunto.* In the making up of a marriage it is not enough that the father gives such or such a one to his son, and his son to her, but there must also be the consent of his son; he must approve and accept the Father's gift. And so does Christ here. He approves and accepts the Father's gift. The Father wills His taking such and such poor sinners to wife, and accordingly gives Him to them and them to Him. And the will of Christ falls in with, and is conformed to, the will of the Father herein and so the match goes on. This you have clearly held forth, John 6:37, "All that the Father hath given Me, come unto Me; and him that cometh to Me, I will in no wise cast out."

Here are, among others, two things:

Here is the Father's giving of poor sinners to Christ, and therein His will and consent that they should be espoused to Him in these words, "All that the Father hath given Me."

Here is Christ's approbation and acceptance of the gift of the Father, with His will and consent to espouse them to Himself in these words, "And him that cometh unto Me I will in no wise cast out"; that is, I will assuredly receive and accept him. I will take him into a conjugal union and relation to myself. Christ here plainly declares His acceptance of the Father's gift, giving poor sinners to Him to be His spouse. It is a great saying, and suitable to this I am speaking, which I have read in a great divine, "The eternal and good pleasure of God precedes; but Christ the bridegroom cannot but will the same thing that the Father wills. His will is conformed to the Father's and, therefore, does He accept us as His spouse."

In a word, in this act of grace Christ's language is such as this, "Father, dost Thou give such and such poor sinners to Me? And is it Thy will that they should be espoused to Me? Content, I do freely accept them, and am willing to espouse them to Myself forever. It is true, they are poor worthless creatures, altogether unsuitable to My dignity and greatness; but, Father, they are Thy gift, and I accept them as such. True, there is no beauty in them that I should desire them, but they are Thy gift and I will marry them and make them beautiful." And O what grace is this!

4. *The Lord Jesus Christ not only approves and accepts the Father's gift, but, moreover, He redeems them thus given to Him with the price of His own blood.* He ransoms them from sin, death, and hell, whereunto, in themselves, they were all in bondage; which also necessarily concurs to the accomplishment of the espousal between Him and them. It is observed by some that in the eastern countries it was the manner for men to buy their wives; and indeed so much seems to be intimated in

that message of Saul to David where, when he would persuade David to marry his daughter, in pretense at least, he sends him word that he desired not any dowry but so and so. It seems, then, that it was usual to expect a dowry. The same also appears by the practice of Shechem, Genesis 34:11-12, where, being in love with Dinah, Jacob's daughter, he offered to give a dowry for her. "Give me but thy damsel to wife, and ask me never so much dowry and gift, and I will give it thee." To be sure, it is so here. Christ buys all His spouses and gives a vast gift for them; Christ indeed is in love with poor sinners given Him by the Father and desires to marry them to Himself; but He must buy them if He means to have them, and buy them He does, and at a dear rate. He gives a great dowry for them, even His life, His blood, His glory, and all for a time. Hence He is said to give Himself for us, and to purchase us by His blood. Hence we are said to be bought by Him with a price, with a great price, with a price of inestimable value, even His own most precious blood.

The case lies thus: The elect, as well as others, were all gone into captivity, sold under sin and Satan, in bondage to death, hell, and wrath, which is the condition of all by nature. And if Christ will have them as His spouse He must ransom and redeem them from all, which accordingly He does. He bleeds, He dies, He gives Himself a ransom for them, in order to marry them to Himself. He had indeed a mind to a spouse from among the children of men and was in love with them from all eternity, as He Himself tells us. And He is so in love with them that He in effect says unto the Father, as Shechem did to Jacob, "Ask me never so much dowry, and I will give it."

"Why, My Son," says the Father, "if Thou wilt have
them and marry them to Thyself, Thou must give Thy
blood, Thy life, for them. Thou must redeem them
from sin, death, and hell, whereto they are in bondage;
which cannot be done by less than by giving Thyself a
ransom for them." All which Christ assents unto and
complies with, and that with delight, freely giving
Himself for them. And O what grace is this! O to give
such a price for such a spouse! A price so great for a
spouse so black and unworthy; this is a glorious grace
indeed!

5. *Christ makes love to them, tenders Himself unto their
embraces, and withal woos them for their acceptance of Him,
and that with the greatest and most affectionate importunity.*
However much it has cost Christ to redeem poor sinners, and however great a dowry He has given for
them, yet they are unwilling to close with Him; they
have no mind, no heart Christward, and so the match
is not likely to be made up unless something further is
done. Therefore, after all, Christ, as one phrases it,
comes a-wooing them, and earnestly solicits them for
their love and acceptance. He importunes them, and
that in such a way as if He were resolved to take no de-
nial. In Ezekiel 16 we read of a time of love—a time,
that is, of Christ's making love to sinners lying in their
blood and gore. And, indeed, Christ has times of love,
times when He makes love and offers Himself with all
His riches and treasures to poor sinners, when His language to them is, "Behold Me, behold Me"; and "Look
upon Me and be ye saved, all ye ends of the earth."
Now He comes and tells over the stories of His love
to them, how much He has done and suffered for

them, how much His desire is towards them, what great
things He will bestow upon them and enstate them
into, and all to win and allure them to Himself, to gain
their love and consent to accept Him, and to be His in
a marriage covenant.

Time was when Christ came and did this in person,
when He stood and cried, "If any man thirst, let him
come unto Me and drink." Time was when He impor-
tuned poor sinners from day to day. He made love to
them time after time, as He did to Jerusalem, Matthew
23:37. For some years together He wooed them and offered Himself and His grace to them in His own Person. And though He does not now come in person, yet,
as David sent his servants to Abigail to commune with
her and to acquaint her with his purpose and desire to
take her to wife, so Christ sends His servants, His ministers, to poor sinners to commune with them and to
declare the love and purposes of His heart towards
them, and to woo them for Him. And as ambassadors
for Christ, we woo poor souls and in Christ's stead we
beseech them to be reconciled to God, to give up their
names and souls to Christ in a marriage covenant. And,
because we can prevail nothing, by and of ourselves,
upon the spirits of men in this great matter, Christ
over and above sends His own blessed Spirit to woo
them and gain upon them, making them willing in the
day of His power.

And this leads me to the consideration of those
other acts of grace in this business wherein the Father
and Jesus Christ work by the Spirit in us and upon us
for the making up of the match between Christ and us.
Only, by the way, let us still see and admire the grace of
Jesus Christ to poor sinners. O that He should woo

such poor vile creatures as we are, and make love to us! Should you see a king, a great king, wooing a beggar, coming now Himself in person, and then sending His servants to her to solicit and importune her love, you would look on this to be great grace. But O this is nothing to the grace of Christ in condescending to woo such as we are—sinners lying in our blood!

Chapter 5

Which gives an account of those more near acts of grace which the Father and Jesus Christ, by the Spirit, do put forth in us and upon us, for the effecting of the espousals between Christ and us

Divine grace has not yet done its work; no, there are other acts which it does and must put forth if ever the marriage is made up between Christ and us. And these I call more near because they are wrought in us and upon us, and more immediately conduce to tying the marriage knot between Christ and the soul; and as, in the former, the Father and Jesus Christ wrought more immediately of and by themselves, so, in these, the blessed Spirit's influence comes in and His grace shows itself, they in these acting by Him. And, the truth is, the match is all this while but half made; but now God comes and, by His Spirit working in and upon the soul, carries on and completes it, which He does by these five acts of grace:

1. *The soul is, by the Spirit of God, divorced from its old husband, the law, and thereby is fitted and prepared for an espousal to Christ.* Naturally we are all married to another husband, even to the law, and we must be divorced from that, or we can never be married and espoused to Christ. So much the Apostle clearly holds forth, "Wherefore, my brethren, ye also are become dead to the law by the body of Christ, that ye should be

married to another, even to Him who is raised from
the dead, that we should bring forth fruit unto God."
Pray, mark the phrase "married to another." The law
then was their husband to which they were married;
and they must be dead to and divorced from that husband if ever they would be married to Jesus Christ.
"Look," says he, for it is His own argument and allu-
sion, "as a woman cannot be the wife of two husbands
at once (but her present husband must be dead before
she can be married to another), so neither can a soul
be espoused to these two husbands at once, the law
and Christ; but he must be dead to or divorced from
the one ere he can be married to the other."

Observe, "Ye are dead to the law." What is it to be
dead to the law? To be dead to the law is to have no
hope, no expectation of life and righteousness by the
law; it is to be sensible that the law cannot save us. Yet
there is more in it than this. To be dead to the law is to
see ourselves dead by the law, to see ourselves lost and
condemned by the law for sin as the transgression
thereof. And thus we must be all dead to or divorced
from the law or we cannot be married to Christ. Now
this the Spirit of God effects by a work of the law upon
the conscience. He divorces the soul from the law by
the law, that is, by bringing home the law to the conscience. This the Apostle felt in his own soul, "I
through the law," says he, "am dead to the law." So
again, "I was alive without the law once; but when the
commandment came, sin revived, and I died." I was
alive without the law once, that is, I thought myself to
be alive. I apprehended my state to be good and
happy, but this was without the law, or before the Spirit
of God by the ministry of the law convinced me of my

sin and misery. Therefore, it follows, when the commandment came, sin revived and I died. That is, when
the law came in its convincing power through the
Spirit upon my soul, then I saw my sinful, dead, and
miserable state. Thus was he himself divorced from the law that he
might be married to Christ. The sum is this: The Spirit
of God comes and shows the soul the strictness and holiness, the purity and spirituality of the law, and makes
him sensible, how large the duty is that it requires, how
impossible it is for him to keep it, and how many ways
he has broken it. He withal lets him see the dreadful-
ness of that curse and condemnation it has justly laid
him under for the breach thereof, and thus he is divorced from it. And this is all one with the Spirit's convincing us of sin and our lost and miserable condition
by reason thereof, which is His first work in order to
faith, and so to our espousing to Christ. Thus, by the
Spirit of God, the soul is divorced from the law; he is
taken off from all expectations of life and happiness by
that and is made to see his own sinfulness, and so his
infinite need of Christ, whereby he is fitted for this
other and better Husband.

2. *The soul being thus divorced from the law and so fitted
and prepared for Christ, then the Spirit of God reveals and offers the Lord Jesus Christ in the promise of the Gospel as a better Husband to him.* Now the blessed Spirit comes and
does as Abraham's servant did, who was sent to take a
wife for Isaac. He told Rebekah of his master's greatness, of his flocks and his herds, his silver and his gold,
his men-servants and his maid-servants, and withal, that
he had given all to Isaac; so the Spirit of God now sets

before the soul the riches and greatness, the beauty and the excellency of the Lord Jesus Christ. He tells them what a full, what a sweet, what a rich, what an amiable one He is and, withal, tenders him to His embraces; He reveals and offers Him to him as one full of grace and truth, as one that has all fullness dwelling in Him, all fullness of life and peace, of righteousness and salvation, as One every way able to save him to the very utmost, which is that which Christ calls His "convincing the world of righteousness." He reveals and offers Him to him in the transcendent beauty, excellency, and amiableness of His person on the one hand, and in the glorious fullness, largeness and sufficiency of His grace and righteousness on the other hand. Thus, I say, He reveals and offers Christ unto the soul, opens His glory, and causes it to shine before him so that now the soul sees in Christ that fullness, that beauty, that love, that amiableness, that sweetness which he never saw before.

Now the soul, as those, "behold His glory, as the glory of the only begotten Son, full of grace and truth"; yea, not only does He thus reveal Christ unto the soul, but fixes the soul's eye upon Him. He makes him to pore and gaze upon Christ as the most excellent and amiable object, and as one infinitely needful for him, and this is called "a seeing of the Son," and that in order to believing; "whosoever seeth the Son, and believeth on Him, shall have everlasting life." The blessed Spirit deals by the soul herein as God, by the angel, did with Hagar, Genesis 21:19, where 'tis said He "opened her eyes," and she saw a well of water for her relief. She was in a very distressed condition, full of bitterness, she and her child both in a perishing condition, being in the wilderness and her water in the bottle being spent; now God shows her a well of water whence she fetches a full supply. So here the poor soul, having been under the convincing power of the law, sees himself in a woeful, miserable, distressed condition, whereupon he is full of bitterness, crying out with Hagar, "How shall I see the child die? How can I bear it to perish eternally?" But now, the Spirit of God comes and opens his eyes and shows him Christ, and Christ as infinitely suitable to him.

"Look," says the Spirit to the soul, being now desolate and undone, "look, here is a Savior for you, a Husband for you, another and a better husband than the law could ever have been, even the Lord Jesus Christ, who is infinitely able to pay all your debts, to supply all your wants, to heal all your wounds, to relieve all your distresses, to pardon all your sins, to satisfy all your desires, to answer all your love, and to give you perfect happiness and satisfaction in and with Himself forever. Look, here He is in the promise; here He is in the covenant; here He is in the tender and invitation of the gospel; here He is at the very door of the heart knocking and calling for admission thereinto; here He is with His arms wide open to receive and embrace you; and that, notwithstanding all your vileness, sinfulness, and unworthiness. Look, therefore, to Him and be saved."

3. *With this offer and revelation of Christ unto the soul, the Spirit of God comes and works a secret love and longing in the soul after Christ.* He does not make a naked offer and revelation of Christ only to the soul, for that would not be enough, but He gives him a secret touch whereby

he is made to breathe and long after Christ, to move a little Christward. He drops a little myrrh upon the handle of the lock, as it were, whereby he is drawn out in holy longings and breathings after sweet Jesus (as you know the case sometimes was with the spouse), and this the Scripture calls a "hungering and thirsting after Christ," Matthew 5:6, and frequently elsewhere. Yea, such is that secret touch which, in and with those offers and revelations of Christ, the Spirit of God gives the soul as that, like that of the loadstone to the needle which sets it a trembling, and will not suffer it to rest until it stands fully pointed Christward, yea, till it finds itself in the very bosom and embraces of that beloved. It is, indeed, such as, by degrees, makes the soul sick of love and longings after Christ, and he cries out for Christ as Rachel sometimes did for children. "Give me children," said she, "or else I die."

"So give me Christ," says the soul, "or else I die. I perish, and that forever." In a word, nothing but Christ will satisfy him. Send him to the creatures; send him to his own duties and services; send him to his highest accomplishments and attainments; and, without Christ, they will not do. Yea, all these he accounts but as dung that he may win Christ, Philippians 3:8. Indeed, heaven and earth, with all the fullness of both, are nothing to him without Christ and a union with Christ. His language now is, "O Christ! Christ above ten thousand worlds! O that Christ were mine! O that I had union with Him! O that I were in His embraces! And O how happy should I be could I call Him mine!" This, I say, is His language. And once it comes to this, then things work well indeed. Then the match is in good forwardness, there being but a hair's breadth, as it were, between Christ and the soul. Therefore:

4. *The soul, being thus inclined Christward, and drawn forth in holy longings after union and communion with Him, the Spirit of God comes and enables him to believe.* He carries the soul to Christ in a way of believing whereby he actually closes with Him and is espoused unto Him. For, my beloved, it is faith which ties the marriage knot and makes up the marriage union between Christ and us. Hence, Christ is said to dwell in our hearts by faith, Ephesians 3:17. Christ's dwelling in our hearts denotes the nearest union and communion between Him and us. And how does He come thus to dwell in our hearts? Why, by faith, by our believing on Him. Hence also Christ tells us that he that eats His flesh and drinks His blood dwells in Him and He in him, John 6:56. By eating Christ's flesh and drinking His blood is meant our believing on Him; and so He Himself expounds it, for He makes eating and drinking of Him, and believing on Him, all one throughout the chapter. Now, says He, "he that eateth My flesh, and drinketh My blood, dwelleth in Me, and I in Him," that is, "he has the nearest union and communion with Me." It is faith, then, you see, that unites and so espouses us to Christ. Faith gives Christ an inlet into the soul and it gives the soul an inlet into Christ. And so they are made one and married together.

By believing we consent to take Christ and actually take Him for our only Head and Husband forever; and so the match is made up between Him and us. "We, by faith," says a learned man, "wrought in us by the Holy Spirit, consent unto this marriage with Christ." Christ, as you heard before, consents thereunto, as God consented hereunto from all eternity; and, as man, He consents hereunto in time. For, as divines observe, Christ has a double will: His divine and human. With the first He consented to His espousal from eternity; with the second He consents hereunto in time and never changes therein. Now, as Christ gives His consent, so we must also give ours, which we do by believing in Him, by which the match is made up between Him and us.

The Threefold Act of Faith

Now, there is a threefold act of faith which the Spirit of God works in the soul, whereby he more especially closes with Christ and is espoused unto Him, made one with Him in a marriage covenant: (1) An act of choice or election; (2) An act of trust or dependence; and (3) An act of resignation or subjection.

1. An act of choice or election. In the act or work of believing, the soul is, by the Spirit of God, made solemnly and deliberately to choose Christ as his only Head and Husband, his Lord and Savior, being thus offered to him in the gospel. Choice, or election, as the schoolmen tell us, is an act of the will whereby it pitches upon some one thing and prefers that before all others in order to such or such an end. Accordingly, we may conceive of this act of faith we are speaking of as lying thus: the will is, by the Spirit of God, sweetly and powerfully determined upon Christ, preferring Him for a Head and Husband, a Lord and Savior, before all others. It singles Him out, as it were, from all others, whether persons or things in heaven or earth,

and embraces Him as the best Husband, the best Savior, the best Lord. There are others who make love to him and offer themselves to his embraces, such as sin, self, the law, and the world with its enticements; but he passes by all, yea, rejects all with loathing and indignation, and pitches upon Christ as infinitely best, saying to Him, "I will have none in heaven but Thee, and there is none upon earth that I desire in comparison with Thee." This the Scripture calls sometimes a "laying hold upon Christ," sometimes "a receiving or embracing of Christ." It is true, in the work of faith, Christ is and must be received into the understanding, but He is most properly said to be received into our will and affections. Christ in the gospel is revealed and offered to the soul with all His riches, fullness, and perfections; He is tendered to him as a full, a mighty, and uttermost Savior; as one who has not only an infinite fullness and sufficiency in Him to redeem and save, but also an infinite suitableness and amiableness in Him to endear and delight the soul.

And, accordingly, the soul accepts and embraces Him; he cleaves to Him and fastens upon Him, resolving to have none but Him alone. His language of Him now is, "There is none like Christ; no Head like this Head; no Husband like this Husband; no Savior like this Savior for my soul. This is the Head, the Husband, the Savior that I need and that, indeed, my soul desires. No love like His love; no beauty like His beauty; no blood like His blood; no righteousness like His righteousness; no fulness like His fulness. He therefore, and He alone, shall be my Head, my Husband, my Savior, and my all forever. Sweet Jesus, dost Thou tender Thyself for a Head and Husband to me? And

art Thou willing to be embraced by me? Lo, then, I do
with my whole soul accept Thee, and that for all times
and in all conditions, with all Thy holiness as well as
Thy love, with all Thy inconveniences as well as Thy
privileges, to suffer for Thee as well as to reign with
Thee." And this the soul does upon the deepest counsel and most mature deliberation. And, accordingly, he
abides by his choice forever.

    2. An act of trust or dependence. As in the work of
faith the soul is, by the Spirit of God, made to choose
Christ, so also it is made to trust and depend upon
Him for all grace, righteousness, and salvation. Now, it
bottoms upon Christ, anchors upon Christ, rests and
relies upon Christ for all life and peace, for all grace
on earth and glory in heaven. He lays the whole weight
and stress of his salvation upon Him; he commits all to
Him, ventures all upon Him, expects all from Him.
This the Scripture calls sometimes "a trusting in
Christ," sometimes "a leaning on Christ," sometimes "a
hoping in Christ," and in this respect Christ is called
"our hope." Our hope, that is, the object of our hope
and trust as to life and salvation. The soul has no hope
in itself; no hope in the creature; no hope in the law or
first covenant; no hope in anything in heaven or on
earth on this side of Christ. He looks here and there,
to this and to that, but he can find no solid ground of
hope, no bottom to build or rest upon for life and salvation; but then he turns his eye upon Christ, and
there he sees abundant ground of hope. He beholds
Him upon the cross and there is hope; he beholds
Him upon the throne and there is hope; he looks
upon Him dying and there is hope; he looks upon
Him rising, ascending, sitting at the Father's right

hand making intercession for us, and there is hope; he looks upon the infinite virtue of His blood, the infinite efficacy of His Spirit, the infinite fullness of His grace, the infinite dimensions of His love, the infinite freeness and faithfulness of His promise; and, in these, he sees infinite ground of hope and trust. And, accordingly, he rests and ventures all upon Him. "Here I will build," says he, "here I will bottom; here I will rest; here I will hang and depend; here I will live. Yea, and if die I must, here I will die."

His language to Christ now is like that of the Psalmist to God in another case, "Now, Lord, what wait I for? My hope is in Thee." This is to "cast anchor within the veil," Hebrews 6:19. And, indeed, it is with poor souls, many times, as with persons at sea: the storm arises; the waves lift up themselves and are beating upon them; they are ready to sink every moment, and their very soul is melted because of heaviness. But soon they sound bottom, cast anchor, and are at rest. So poor souls are under storms of sin, guilt, and wrath, perishing in their own apprehension every moment; but soon they drop an anchor of hope upon Christ, and rest upon Him.

Or it is with them, in this case, as it was with the dove when she was first sent out of the ark. She found no resting place abroad for the sole of her foot, but at length returned to the ark and there found rest. So the poor guilty soul finds no rest anywhere but in Christ. His language in this act of faith is such as this: "I am a poor, lost, sinful, distressed creature, and there is but one door I can expect relief from, and that is Christ,. and at this door I will lie and wait. I know He is able to help me, for He can save to the uttermost; and surely

He has compassion, great compassion, towards poor sinners. He is a merciful High Priest." He says concerning Him, as they sometimes did concerning the King of Israel, "Behold we have heard that the King of Israel is a merciful king, peradventure He will save us. Yea, He has bid me look to Him and be saved; and He invites all them that are weary and heavy laden to come to Him, and promises them rest. Why then should I not rest and rely upon Him? It is true, I am a mighty sinner, but He is a more mighty Savior. Have I sinned to the utmost? He has satisfied to the utmost. What shall I say? True, I am death, but Christ is life. I am darkness, but Christ is light. I am sin, but Christ is holiness. I am guilt, but Christ is righteousness. I am emptiness and nothingness, but Christ is fullness and sufficiency. I have broken the law, but Christ has fulfilled the law, and His life is infinitely able to swallow up my death; His light, my darkness; His holiness, my sin; His righteousness, my guilt; His fullness, my emptiness. On Him, therefore, I will lean and live and hope. It is true, I am utterly unworthy of any life, any grace, any favor; but Christ does all for sinners freely. He loves freely, He pardons freely, He saves freely. However vile, therefore, and unworthy I am, yet I will rest and depend upon Him. Who knows but He may cast an eye of love upon me? This is that act of faith which is held forth, Isaiah 45:24, 'Surely, shall one say, in the Lord have I righteousness and strength.' I have neither strength nor righteousness of my own, but I have all righteousness and strength in Christ—all righteousness for pardon and justification and all strength for holiness and sanctification. This is what the Apostle calls a 'rejoicing in Christ Jesus, having no confidence in the flesh.' "

To draw towards a conclusion of this head, which-
ever way the soul looks on this side of Christ, it meets
with nothing but discouragement. If he looks to himself, he sees nothing but sin and guilt, blackness and
deformity! In his heart he sees a fountain of sin, an
abyss of sin, a very hell of sin and wickedness; in his life
he finds innumerable evils, sins of a crimson dye and
scarlet tincture, staring him in the face; yea, his very
duties are not without sin. Even in these, there is an
abundance of pride, formality, unbelief, and the like;
his very righteousness is as filthy rags. If he looks unto
the law, he reads his doom and condemnation in every
line thereof; there he finds himself under the curse;
and there he sees nothing but fear and blackness and
darkness and tempests. If he looks to justice, he finds it
to be a flaming sword keeping him from the tree of
life, from all happiness. Justice appears with an angry,
frowning countenance, demanding satisfaction, as being infinitely wronged; but now, in the midst of all
these discouragements, the poor soul at length gets a
sight of Christ, in whom he sees encouragement after
all. He discovers land in a storm, as it were, and finds
in Him a bottom to rest his weary spirit upon. In Him,
he sees that which can atone to God, satisfy justice, answer all the demands of the law, fully deliver him from
sin and guilt, and make him both holy and happy forever; and, accordingly, he rests and rolls himself upon
Him, resolving that, if he dies, he will thus die leaning
upon this Beloved.

3. An act of resignation or subjection. As in the
work of faith the soul thus chooses Christ and depends
upon Him, so also he is, by the Spirit of God, made
cordially and unreservedly to resign up himself unto

Him, to be ruled, governed, and disposed of by Him in
His own way. The soul now puts himself out of his own
power and possession; he passes himself away for himself; and he gives up himself into the power and possession of Jesus Christ to be ruled, governed, and saved
by Him as He sees good; which is properly that act of
faith which we call resignation. And this the Scripture
often mentions, "One shall say, I am the Lord's," that
is, he shall give or resign up himself to the Lord to be
forever His and at His disposal. So, 2 Corinthians 8:5,
"They gave themselves unto the Lord"; and Ephesians
5:24, the church is said to be "subject to Christ." The
case seems to be this: there having many treaties
passed in order to a match between Christ and the
soul, the soul at length, through the help of the Divine
Spirit, is made freely to consent to take Christ for his
only Head and Husband, and to be subject to Him in
all things, to be perfectly and eternally at His disposal.
His language now to Christ is like that of Ahab to
Benhadad, "Behold I am thine, and all that I have is
thine."

"Sweet Lord Jesus," says the soul, "I have been my
own, and have lived too much in my own will and to
my own ends and interests; but now I desire to be
Thine, and to live in Thy will, and to Thine ends. Take
possession of me; save me; rule me; lead me; dispose of
me as Thou pleasest. Do all Thy pleasure in me; pull
down and set up what Thou wilt. I will be, do, and suffer, what Thou wilt have me to be, do, and suffer."

And this is properly that act of faith whereby we
close with Christ as a Lord and King, and is, indeed,
the evidence of the two former. For you must know,
that though faith's first aspect is to Christ as a Savior,

yet it comes to eye Him as a Lord and King also. As faith fully bottoms upon the satisfaction of Christ, so it freely bows to the scepter of Christ. Yea, when faith cannot challenge Christ as a Savior, yet it will own Christ as a Lord. You know how Laban spake to Abraham's servant upon sight of the earrings and bracelets which he had given his sister Rebecca and upon his hearing a relation from her of his discourse with her, "Come in thou blessed of the Lord, why standest thou without? I have room for thee." In like manner does the soul speak to Christ upon the sight of that worth that is in Him, and that need which he has of Him. "Come in, thou blessed of the Lord. Come in, thou blessed of the Lord. Why standest thou without? I have room for Thee in my understanding, and in my will and affections; and I would have Thee possess all and command all."

In a word, the soul freely gives up himself to Christ's holy and spiritual government. "Thou art a holy Christ," says he, "He who is to reign. I resign up myself to Thee. I will have no Lord but Thee. Take the whole throne to Thyself within me. I know Thy yoke is an easy yoke and I desire to bear it. Thy scepter is a righteous scepter and I desire to bow to it. Thy kingdom is a kingdom of righteousness, peace, and joy in the Holy Ghost, and I heartily desire to come under the power of it. I would be sanctified as well as justified. I desire Thy Spirit to subdue my corruptions for me and to make me holy as well as Thy blood to wash away my guilt for me and ingratiate me with Thyself." And this is what the Scripture calls an opening of the gates and lifting up of the everlasting doors to let Christ the King of Glory in. Thus, by these three, which indeed are the great uniting acts of faith, the Spirit of God enables the soul to close with Christ in a marriage covenant and relation.

5. *The soul, being thus enabled to believe, closes with Christ in a marriage covenant; then, as the crown and perfection of all, the blessed Spirit of God takes up His abode and dwells forever in that soul as the pledge and everlasting bond of this marriage union and relation between them.* The sweet Spirit not only comes as a friend to treat about the match, and also to tie the marriage knot between Christ and us; but moreover, this being done, He remains Himself in the soul as a love-token from Christ to him, as the pawn and pledge of this espousal, and as the everlasting bond and confirmation of this marriage union and relation. Hence that statement of the Apostle, "He that is joined to the Lord, is one spirit"; one spirit with the Lord he is joined to. That Spirit which joined him to Christ remains in him and in Christ both. Christ leaves His own Spirit in His spouses as the pledge and bond of that marriage union that is between Him and them so that He and they have the same Spirit dwelling in them. Yet, with this difference, He dwells in Christ without measure, in us by measure; in Christ immediately, by virtue of the personal union, in us by His gifts and graces; in Christ as a Head, in us as members; and He, with these, are the love tokens, the pawns and pledges of His marriage-troth, plighted between Christ and us. And this, indeed, is that which makes this union so strong and inviolable that it can never be broken. Yea, not only does He remain in the soul as the pledge and bond of this union, but also decks and adorns the soul with grace to make him

ready for the consummation of the marriage above.
You know that when Abraham's servant saw that
Rebecca consented to be Isaac's wife, he then gave her
jewels of silver, jewels of gold, and rich raiment. So the
blessed Spirit of God, having gained the soul's consent
to be espoused to Christ, and the marriage knot being
tied between them, now He dwells in the soul to deck
and adorn him. Now He gives him jewels of gold and
silver, furnishes and beautifies him with all divine and
heavenly graces. He dwells in him as an indeficient
spring and fountain of all grace and gracious dispositions till He has lodged him safe in the arms and bosom of his sweet Husband above.

Thus, at length, the espousal or marriage relation is
made up between Christ and the soul. And O how
blessed is the soul that is thus espoused to Him! I must
say to such a soul, "Blessed be the day that ever you
were born; blessed the womb that bore you, and
blessed the breasts at which you sucked; blessed gospel
which revealed this sweet Christ to you, and blessed
Spirit that has tied this happy knot between Him and
you!"

Chapter 6

Being a call to, and treaty with, souls, in order to an espousal between Christ and them

Well, what is the meaning of all this? Surely it should have a mighty influence upon the spirits of men to draw and allure them to Christ, to induce them at least to look after an acquaintance with this blessed espousal to Him. And, indeed, I would take occasion hence to treat with eternal souls in order to a match between Christ and them; and O that I could do it effectually! Look, my beloved, as David sent his servants to Abigail to commune with her in order to his taking her to wife, so has the Lord Jesus sent me, his poor unworthy servant, to you this day to commune with you in order to the espousing of you to Himself. And O that you would do in this case as she did in that, for "she hastened," it is said, "and arose and went to David, and she became his wife." O that you would arise, arise out of your sins, arise out of your unbelief, arise out of your carnal security, and go to Christ, and become His spouse! And, not only so but, as she did, make haste in the business; close speedily with Him, even today. O blessed day, might I succeed as they did! How happy would it be for you! How comfortable for me! And how joyful for us all in the day of the Bridegroom's coming!

Sirs, let me say, O that I might say of you, as Paul of

his Corinthians, here, "I have espoused you to one
Husband, even to Christ." And why should it not be
thus? Why should you not rise and go with me to sweet
Jesus and be espoused unto Him? Can you make light
of all that love, that comfort, that sweetness, that happiness, that blessed union and communion, that delight, solace, and complacency of soul which this espousal carries in it? Or, is there anything can make up
the loss of these? Can sin and the creature afford anything comparable hereunto? Surely, there is more
sweetness, more happiness, in one kiss of the mouth of
this blessed Lord, in one embrace in His bosom, one
moment's communion with Him, than in all the delights of sin and the creature. If you doubt it, come
and see. Experienced souls will tell you that one descent of love from Christ, one beam of the light of His
countenance, one turn with Him in His galleries, is infinitely beyond all earthly delights whatsoever. Again,
can you be content to die and perish eternally, rather
than live and be made happy in such a sweet and desirable way as this of being espoused to Christ is? A
more sweet and desirable way of being made happy
than this of an espousal to Christ, surely, neither men
nor angels could have ever thought on. And can you,
O eternal souls, be content to die, to perish, to be
damned and miserable forever, rather than be saved
and made happy this way? If you get not union with,
and a marriage relation to, this sweet Lord, you must
die and perish for ever. "Know you not," says the
Apostle, "that Jesus Christ is in you, except ye be reprobates?" If Christ is not in us, we are certainly reprobates; we are rejected of God and out of His favor, and
then, surely, we must perish.

Naturally, we are all dead, all lost, all condemned. "Judgment came upon all men to condemnation," Romans 5:18; and "we are all the children of wrath," Ephesians 2:3. And if ever we are justified and saved, it must be by a marriage union and relation to Christ. "There is no condemnation," says the Apostle, or, as the words are, "nothing of condemnation to them that are in Christ Jesus." But, as is there implied, there is nothing *but* condemnation to them that are out of Christ Jesus. Once more, can you be content to be shut out from the marriage at last forever? Think of that Scripture, and bear the dread of it if you can, Matthew 25:10, "And they that were ready went in to the marriage and the door was shut," shut against others who then would fain enter. To be shut out from the marriage supper at last is to be shut out from God, from Christ, from the Comforter, from all the saints and angels, from all happiness, yea, and from all hopes of happiness forever. And thus you must expect to be shut out from the marriage at last if you do not come into an espousal to Him here. And do you think that you can bear it? Can you be content to hear Christ say unto you at last, "Depart from Me, depart. You would have none of Me on earth though I wooed and sought you with tears. And, therefore, now you shall have none of Me in heaven. You might have been happy in a union and communion with Me, and the arms of My love were open to have received you, but you would not. Therefore, now, depart from Me, I know you not." And can you bear this?

Besides, what is it that keeps your soul from closing with Christ in this marriage relation? A vain world, a filthy lust, a painful, perishing pleasure, a sensual appetite; and are these better than Christ? Are these, indeed, things to be laid in the balance by you against Christ, yea, and to weigh Him down in your value? O monstrous stupidity!

In short, sirs, the matter I am treating with you about is no trifle; it is of no less moment and importance to you than eternal life or death, eternal salvation or damnation, comes to. Your eternal all depends upon it, for you must live or die, be saved or damned eternally, according as you do or do not close with Christ in a marriage union and relation here. Why, then, should you stand off from Him? Yea, why should not this be the day of espousals between Him and you? O be not shy, be not coy to Christ but embrace His love. Surely, His arms are wide open to receive you. His heart is upon you and His desire is towards you. Lift up, therefore, the everlasting doors and let the King of Glory in. Give up your names and souls unto Him forever.

Some of you are young and have your affections green and fresh. O that you would go with me to sweet Jesus and become His spouse. You cannot love Him nor be married to Him too soon. O let Him have your hearts before this world has defiled and debauched them! Others of you are older and have withstood the calls and offers of Christ long; yet lo, He once more offers Himself to you. O now close with Him and all will be well yet!

But, for the better succeeding of this treaty, I shall, in the managing of it, speak to three things.

First, I will show you what manner of Husband the Lord Jesus Christ is, and how He is qualified so as to render Him desirable in that relation.

Second, I will show you what great things He does
for all His spouses.

Third, I will show you how much His heart is upon
a match with you. And now, as Abraham's servant,
when he was going to get a wife for Isaac, prayed, saying, "O Lord God of my master, Abraham, send me
good speed this day," so would I, upon the bended
knees of my soul pray, "O Lord God, the God and
Father of my Royal Master, Jesus Christ, send me good
speed this day that I may win, through Thy grace, a
spouse for Him."

Chapter 7

Which shows what manner of Husband Christ is, and how qualified for the endearing of Him to souls, and rendering Him desirable in a conjugal union

What is thy beloved more than another beloved, that thou dost so charge us?" So the Daughters of Jerusalem spake unto the spouse, Song of Solomon 5:9. In like manner may some say unto me, "Who or what is this Christ that you so press us to an espousal with Him? What is there in Him to render Him desirable to us? Who or what is He?" Truly I cannot tell; nor could I had I the tongue of men and angels. And I am almost afraid to speak of Him, lest I should darken His glory instead of displaying it. This I am sure of: He is, as one speaks of Him, earth's wonder and heaven's wonder both, and has all that in Him, and that in infinite eminency and perfection, that should render Him grateful and desirable to souls in a conjugal relation. Look therefore upon Him, and view Him a little, and see if there is anything you can desire in such a relation that is wanting in Him. I will lay this more fully before you in these following particulars.

1. *Are you for dignity and greatness?* This goes far among men, and makes many a match. For this, there is none like Christ; none so great, so glorious, so honorable as He. Pray, view Him a little. As to His descent, He came forth from God by eternal generation and is

the eternal Son of the eternal Father. View Him in His person, and there you will see nothing but greatness; for He is no other than God-man, and has all the excellencies of both natures in one person. He is Emmanuel, God with us, God in our nature. He is God, the True God, the Great God, the Mighty God, God over all, or the Most High God, God equal with the Father, having the same divine essence and essential perfections in Him that the Father has in Him. He is the brightness of the Father's glory and the express character of His person; one in whom the whole majesty, luster, and glory of the Father shines forth; one in whom the Father has engraven all His eternal excellencies. Some small beams and rays of God's glory shine forth in the saints and angels, but in Christ the fullness, luster, and brightness of it appears. View Him in His office and relation with the dignity that even here He is advanced unto. He is a king, a great king, King of Kings, and Lord or Lords; King of saints, King of nations, King of glory. He is the Head of all principalities and powers; and it is their glory that they have such a Head. He is the fellow of the Lord of Hosts; He is the Firstborn of God, higher than the kings of the earth; He is set down at God's own right hand in heavenly places, far above all principalities, and powers, and might, and dominion. He is made higher than the heavens.

Among all persons, and in all things, whether in heaven or earth, He has the pre-eminence; such is His greatness that the whole creation is bound to perform homage and worship to Him, the angels themselves not excepted. "Let all the angels of God worship Him," says the Father, and "God hath highly exalted Him, and given Him a name above every name, that at the name of Jesus every knee should bow, of things in heaven and things on earth, and things under the earth"; that is, angels as well as men must perform worship to Him. And, indeed, a refusal so to do would turn angels into devils. He is beloved, feared, believed on, obeyed, prayed unto, praised, admitted, and delighted in by all. He is to have equal honor with the Father. All must honor the Son as they honor the Father.

What shall I say? He has the sovereign lordship and disposal both of grace and glory in His hand: "the Son quickeneth whom He will." He says unto one, "Live," and he lives; and to another, "Live," and he lives; and the rest of the dead live not. "He has the keys of death and hell." He has the government of the whole world in His hand. "His kingdom ruleth over all." He is in full possession of a kingdom over the whole creation, all judgment being committed to Him. And O how glorious is He in the whole of it! Glorious in His throne, which is at the right hand of God; glorious in His commission, which is all power in heaven and earth; glorious in His scepter, which is a scepter of righteousness; glorious in His attendants, more than a thousand times ten thousand of His holy ones, even thousands of angels; glorious in His way of rule, full of grace and sweetness towards His people, full of terror and majesty towards His enemies, His arrows being sharp in their hearts.

And, as He governs all now, so He will judge all at last; and all must stand or fall, live or die, be saved or damned forever, according to what sentence He shall pass upon them. O how great is this Lord! And how

worthy to be embraced by us! O, sirs, will you deny so
great, so glorious a Person when He makes love to you?
Should you see some great prince wooing a beggar in
rags upon the dunghill, you would wonder to see her
slight him and make him wait time after time upon
her. Why, there is an infinitely greater Person than the
greatest of kings that woos and solicits you for love;
and will you yet be shy of Him and make Him wait?
Will you refuse Him? Then wonder at your own sordid
ingratitude.

2. *Are you for riches and treasures?* This weighs with
most. For this, there is none like Christ; He has riches
as well as greatness to recommend Him to you; "riches
and honor are with Me." Yea, and His riches are the
best sort. His are spiritual riches, "treasures in heaven";
riches of life and love, peace and pardon, grace and
glory, righteousness and salvation; riches *of* glory and
riches *in* glory. And O what poor things are the riches
of this world to these! His are true riches. The riches of
this world are but painted riches; His are substantial
riches. "I will cause them that love Me to inherit substance." The riches of this world are vain; they are not.
The riches of Christ have a reality in them; His are lasting and durable riches. "Riches and honor are with
Me, yea, durable riches and righteousness." Worldly
riches are perishing and uncertain things; now we enjoy them, but, all of a sudden, they are gone and dis-
appear; but Christ's are eternal riches for an eternal
soul. And as His riches are thus of the best sort, so He
has great abundance of them. His riches are boundless
and unsearchable. "To me," says St. Paul, "it is given to
preach the unsearchable riches of Christ." He is heir of

all things; all the treasures of heaven and earth are His; He has all fullness dwelling in Him, even all the fullness of the Godhead; whole God dwells in Him.

He has enough to supply all our wants and to answer all our desires. Do we want grace? He is full of grace. Do we want life? With Him is the fountain of life. Do we want redemption, redemption from sin, from death, from hell, from wrath? With Him is plenteous redemption. Do we want peace? He gives peace; "My peace I give unto you." Do we want righteousness? "He has fulfilled all righteousness," and He has become "the Lord our righteousness." Now, will you reject this right Lord? You are poor, miserable, and naked; and will you not embrace this Christ offering Himself with all these riches towards you? O how justly then will you perish for ever! O that there were some covetous soul here this day that would be taken with the riches of Christ!

3. *Are you for bounty, for a noble and generous spirit?* That is desirable in such a relation, and takes much with many; for this also, there is none like Christ. He is a bountiful Lord, or a noble and generous spirit, as well as rich. Many a man has riches enough, but has a base, narrow, covetous spirit, and so his wife has little of them; but Christ has a noble, generous, bountiful heart. He is not only rich, but He is also willing to lay out His riches and treasures upon His spouses; all the treasures of His love and grace, all the treasure of His righteousness and consolation. He would have them abundantly filled, abundantly comforted, abundantly enriched forever. What a generous spirit towards them does He express, Song of Solomon 5:1, "Eat, O friends,

drink, yea, drink abundantly, O beloved." As if He
should say, "I have enough, infinitely enough, for you,
and I would have you to have enough. I would have
you have your souls full of all good." He would have
them to have full graces, full joys, full comforts, and
full happiness, for ever. "These things speak I unto
you," says He, "that your joy may be full"; and again,
"Ask that you may receive, that your joy may be full."
He wills them like happiness with Himself; like love
and embraces in the Father's bosom; like grace and
holiness. O what a noble, generous, bountiful heart
has this sweet Lord towards His spouse! Soul, shall it
not draw and allure you to Him? Nothing will satisfy
Him less than their participating with Him in His own
blessedness. Soul, if you reject this bountiful Lord,
know that He has treasures of wrath and vengeance
also which He will plentifully pour out upon you for
ever.

4. *Are you for wisdom and knowledge?* Wisdom and
knowledge render a person lovely and desirable; it is,
indeed, one of a person's highest excellencies and perfections. For this also there is none like Christ. He is
the wisdom of God, and the power of God; the infinite
wisdom of the eternal God shines forth in Him and
through Him; yea, "in Him are hid all the treasures of
wisdom and knowledge"; which may be understood ac-
tively as well as passively, He knowing all, as well as having all that is worth knowing in Him. He is the only
wise God. There is no true wisdom but in Him, and
there is no true wisdom to be had but by Him and
from Him. He is often in Scripture called "Wisdom," to
denote that infinite wisdom that is in Him. He knows

all persons and all things. He knows the Father and He
is known of Him. He knows the mind and will of the
Father; hence He is said to be in His bosom, which is
the place of secrets as well as love. He knows all His
Father's counsels and decrees, which have been of old,
touching the salvation and damnation of man. Hence
we read of the Lamb's Book of Life and names written
therein. He knows all the works of God the Father.
"The Father loveth the Son, and showeth Him whatsoever He doth." He knows the attributes and perfections
of God, and He only; He knows the whole Word of
God, being Himself the Word.

It is observed by one that the angels themselves do
not know all the Word of God, but Christ does. And as
He thus knows God and the things of God, so also He
knows man and the things of man. He knows all men,
and what is in them. He knows the state, the spirits, the
frames, the thoughts, the ends, the counsels, the ways,
the wants, the burdens, the temptations of all. In a
word, He is infinite in wisdom and counsel, and He
knows perfectly how to promote His own glory, so how
to defend, save, and comfort His spouses, and carry on
their happiness in the best way. O, who would not have
such a Husband! Soul, if you reject Him, know that His
wisdom will fight against you; and He knows how to
damn and destroy forever.

5. *Are you for beauty?* That takes with most. For this,
there is none like Christ; for beauty and comeliness,
He infinitely surpasses both men and angels. We read
of Moses that He was "exceeding fair," and of David,
that he was "ruddy, and of a beautiful countenance."
And Josephus reports of one of them that all that saw

Him were amazed and enamored of His beauty. O but what was their beauty to Christ's? Were their beauty and, with theirs, the beauty of men and angels put together, it would all be nothing to the beauty of Christ; not so much as the light of a farthing candle is to the light of the sun at noonday. He is beautiful and glorious, Isaiah 4:2. Was Moses fair? Christ is infinitely more fair; He is fairer than the children of men. And had you an eye to behold His beauty, you could not but be amazed at it and enamored of it. Was David ruddy and of a beautiful countenance? See what the spouse says of Christ, Song of Solomon 5:10, "My beloved is white and ruddy, the chiefest among ten thousand"; which notes the perfection of His beauty. And therefore she concludes all with this (having spoken of the beauty of His several parts), "He is altogether lovely"; or, He is all loveliness. As if she should say, "What do I do? There is no end of His beauty and amiableness; there is nothing in Him but what is lovely, and there is nothing lovely but what is in Him. Neither is there anything in the whole creation that has beauty and amiableness enough in it to be a shadow and resemblance of His beauty and amiableness."

"O fair sun," says Rutherford, "and fair moon, and fair stars, and fair flowers, and fair roses, and fair lilies; but O ten thousand times fairer Lord Jesus! Alas, I have wronged Him in making the comparison this way. O black sun and moon! but O fair Lord Jesus! O black flowers and black lilies and roses! but O fair, fair, even fair, Lord Jesus! O black heaven! but O fair Christ! O black angels! but O surpassingly fair Lord Jesus!"

In short, divines observe that there is something in Christ more amiable than salvation. And, indeed, there are those heart-endearing beauties, those soul-ravishing excellencies in the Person of this beloved that are unspeakably beyond salvation itself. He is the brightness, the luster, the shining forth of His Father's glory. O, who would not be ravished with, and enamored of, His beauty? A small sight and report thereof set the daughters of Jerusalem seeking after Him; and shall it have no influence upon you to draw and allure you to Him? Does one so fair and beautiful make love to such black and deformed creatures as you and I are, and shall we refuse Him? O that His beauty might enamor us!

6. *Are you for love as well as loveliness?* For a sweet, kind, loving disposition? This is desirable to all; for this also, none like Christ. He is of a most sweet, loving, tender, affable disposition. He indeed is love itself, kindness itself, tenderness and compassion itself. God is love. His love to His spouses has all dimensions, heights, breadths, depths, lengths, in it; yea, it passes knowledge, which shows the immensity and unmeasurableness of His love. As if He should say of it, "It is higher than heaven and deeper than the sea. It is broader than the orb of the earth and longer than all time, during and throughout eternity; yea, and it passes knowledge." There are two things which exceed our knowledge—our sins and Christ's love. The one is almost boundless, the other is altogether boundless and bottomless. Though a man has never so many accomplishments to commend him, yet if he is of a rough, crabbed, sour disposition, this renders him unacceptable for such a relation. But to all His other perfections, Christ has this added, that He is infinitely lov-

ing as well as lovely, and of a most kind, tender disposition to His spouses. Hence we read in Scripture of His love, His kindness, His meekness, His gentleness, and the like—all noting the admirable sweetness and amiableness of His disposition.

He wept over His very enemies, even them that finally refused Him; yea, He had a kindness for His murderers and prayed for them, and that while they were murdering Him. Yea, and His prayer carried many of them to heaven. O what love, what kindness, then must He have for His spouses? He that has love for enemies, and such love, what must He have for His friends? It is a sweet gloss which one of the ancients has upon the place last quoted, "Father, forgive them, they know not what they do."

"This," says the ancient writer, "is a word becoming the eternal Word, the Word of the eternal Father. He prays not only for His persecutors and reproachers, but even for His murderers, improving all His interest in His Father for them"; saying in effect, "Father, I entreat Thee, by that fatherly love Thou hast for Me, and by which We are one, hear Me for these My murderers, in forgiving of them; own the love of Thy Son, that Thou mayest pardon His enemies." O what kindness does this argue! In a word, His love is as an ocean which has neither brim nor bottom; neither can He be but kind to His. The law, indeed, of kindness, as it is said of the good wife, is in His lips; yea and in His heart and carriage too, all being full of love. O that His love might draw you! Surely no love like His love; none so full, none so free, none so sweet, none so fruitful, none so ravishing, none so lasting. His love, where He loves, never fails, nor can it ever be broken off. "Who shall separate us," says the Apostle, "from the love of Christ?" That is, nothing can separate us from His love. Neither death, nor life, nor angels, nor principalities, nor powers, nor things present, nor things to come, nor height, nor depth, nor any thing else, can do it. "And I think," says a holy man, "His unchangeable love hath said unto me, I defy thee to break Me or change Me." O sirs, experienced souls will tell you how sweet and good and rich Christ's love is. They will tell you that one sight, one taste of it, makes heaven in the soul, that it is better than wine. And will you reject Him and His love too? Will you pour contempt upon so much kindness? O how justly then will you perish under His wrath! He has wrath in Him as well as love. Wrath for enemies as well as love for His spouses; and His wrath is as hot and terrible as His love is sweet and comfortable. Yea, His love will, if rejected by you, turn into wrath, and no wrath like that which is the result of abused love. O, therefore, close with Christ this day.

7. *Are you for a person of esteem, one that is much valued and beloved?* An ingenious soul would desire this; and for this there is none like Christ. As there is none so kind and loving as He, so there is none so much valued and beloved as He. He is beloved by all whose love is worth having. He is highly valued and beloved by all the saints, both in heaven and earth. The saints in heaven admire and adore Him; it is a part of their happiness to love Him and delight in Him forever. And the saints on earth love and value Him above all others whatsoever. He is the dearly beloved of their souls. How often does the spouse call Him her beloved, and her well-beloved? And once and again she declares

herself sick of love to Him. She is enamored of Him. He is indeed the desire of all nations; that is to say, He is whom all the faithful in all nations love, desire, and delight in. Hence also that of the Apostle, "To you that believe He is precious." The saints love and value Christ above all their natural or creature enjoyments, above father and mother, husband and wife and children, houses and lands, and the like. So much is intimated, Matthew 10:37 and 19:29. They love and value Him above all their spiritual attainments, accounting them but as dung for Christ. They love and value Him above their lives, being ready to die for Him. O how dear is Christ to saints? He is also highly valued and beloved by all the holy angels. He is the great object of their love and admiration. Hence He is said to be seen of angels; that is, to be beloved and delighted in by angels. The blessed angels see that in Christ which enamors them of Him and fills them with love to Him and delight in Him; yea, which fills them with perpetual admirings and adorings of Him. Yea, which is more than all this, He is infinitely valued and beloved by God the Father also. The blessed God sees that in Christ whicj renders Him infinitely amiable and desirable in His eye and to His soul, both as Son and as Mediator. He is infinitely dear and precious to the Father; and as He is the Son of God, the Son of the Father, as the Apostle's expression is, so is He the darling and delight of the Father's soul, and was so from all eternity. So much He Himself tells us, Proverbs 8:30. So is He the infinite and eternal favorite of the infinite and eternal Father; so He is one in essence with the Father and, accordingly, must be infinitely dear to the Father. Hence He is said to be in the

Father's bosom, and, as His Son, was so from eternity.
Now the bosom is the seat of love. And this being in
His Father's bosom notes that strong, ardent, intimate
love which the Father has for Him; yea, even as
Mediator, the Father loves Him; yea, He loves Him
with a choice, a single, and an eminent love, with a
love of the highest strain, the choicest excellency, the
sweetest influence, a love that has a stamp of a special
glory upon it. Hence He is called the Beloved. "He
hath made us accepted in the beloved," that is, in
Christ, who is most dear to God. Hence God calls Him
His beloved Son. "This is My beloved Son, in whom I
am well pleased." Yea, He is called the Son of His love;
"He hath translated us into the kingdom of His dear
Son." The Greek is "the Son of His love." Yea, the
Father proclaims Him to be the delight of His soul;
"Behold," says He, "My servant whom I have chosen;
Mine elect, in whom My soul delighteth." What shall I
say? God loves Himself infinitely, and next to Himself
He loves Christ and delights in Him.

It is true, He loves all the works of His hand as
such, and especially rational creatures, and among
them He has a peculiar love for His saints and the holy
angels; but He loves Christ unspeakably more than all.
He, indeed, is first beloved, most beloved, and best
beloved by Him of all others. God, as the schoolmen
observe, loves the very flesh or human nature of Christ
more than all the angels. In a word, He loves Him so as
that He is even ravished with Him; and He cannot but
love all that are in Him or related by covenant to Him;
and that though altogether unlovely in themselves.

Now, sirs, will you not love and embrace this
beloved One? One that is thus valued and beloved by

saints, by angels, and by God the Father? And let me say, One that is hated and despised by none but devils and devilish ones. Souls, if you reject Him whom all the saints and angels love, admire, and adore, then never expect to live with them in the fruition of Him, but reckon upon living with devils and damned spirits in hell forever. If you reject Him whom the Father loves and delights in, then expect to be rejected both by Him and the Father forever. But, soul, rather be prevailed with to love Him too.

8. *Are you for immortality, for one that lives forever?* This added to the rest is desirable, and for this there is none like Christ. Yea, none but Christ. He and He alone is a never-dying Husband. The best Husband here below is mortal and may leave you in a moment, but Christ is immortal. He is the King immortal, eternal, and He only has immortality. He and He only lives forevermore. "Behold, I live for evermore," says He. He will never leave you in the desolate state of widowhood; yea, not only does He live forever Himself, but, moreover, He makes all His spouses to live forever too. So you find, John 11:25-26, "I am the resurrection and the life: he that believeth in Me, though he were dead, yet shall he live; and whosoever liveth and believeth in Me shall never die."

O what a Husband is this! A Husband that lives forever Himself, and that makes His spouses live forever too. He gives all His spouses such a life as never dies, an immortal life. In a word, close with Him, and as He will live forever as thy Husband so shall you live forever as His spouse. O who would not accept such a person? Soul, if you receive Him, know He lives forever to love you, to comfort you, to make you happy in and with Himself. But if you reject Him, know that He lives forever to punish you, to inflict wrath and vengeance upon you, and to make you completely miserable. But O reject Him not!

Thus have I shown you a little what a Husband Christ is to His spouses. And upon the whole I would say to you, as the spouse did to the daughters of Jerusalem, Song of Solomon 5:16, "This is my beloved, and this is my friend." This is He who offers Himself to your embraces. Surely He is no mean, no despicable Person, but One infinitely desirable. Now, what do you say? Will you have Him or will you not? Possibly this is the last offer He will ever make of Himself to you. Possibly the match must be made now or never. Therefore, now, close with Him. Accept Him upon His own terms who surely is worthy of all acceptance.

Chapter 8

Which shows what great things Christ does for all His spouses

Some may say, "True, Christ's person is desirable, but what will He do for His spouses? What may our souls expect from Him in case we should close up with Him in a marriage covenant?"

What will He do? What will He *not* do for you? Surely He acts like Himself and does great things for all His spouses. And O happy, happy they that are indeed espoused unto Him! I shall, for the more effectual drawing of poor souls to Him, show you what He does for His spouses in these following particulars:

1. He pays all their debts.
2. He supplies all their wants.
3. He heals all their maladies.
4. He bears all their burdens.
5. He sweetens all their afflictions.
6. He subdues all their enemies.
7. He minds and manages all their concerns.
8. He joins them in eternal life and glory.

1. *He pays all their debts, fully discharging their souls from all sin and guilt.* No sooner is a woman married to her husband but immediately all her debts become his; he pays all, at least he is liable so to do. In like manner, no sooner is a soul espoused to Christ but all his debts

to law and justice become Christ's and He pays all. And
O how great a thing is this! Friends, we are all in debt
to the law and justice of God. We owe, each one of us,
more than our ten thousand talents. We lie under
whole mountains of sin and guilt. The truth is, our first
father left us and all his posterity in debt. We brought
sin and guilt into the world with us, and the first day
we were born divine justice might have arrested us and
cast us into the dismal prison of utter darkness. "I
came of those parents," says one of the ancients, "who
made me damned before I was born; they, sinners, be-
got me a sinner in their sin." And, to the same purpose, another of them speaks, "No man is free from sin
in the sight of God; no, not an infant of a day old."
And, to give you a greater authority than these, the
holy Apostle asserts the same thing, Romans 5:12, "By
one man sin entered into the world, and death by sin;
and so death passed upon all men, for that all have
sinned." Adam sinned, and we all sinned in him, we all
being in him as a common head; and the guilt of the
act of this sin is as truly ours as if we had, each one of
us, acted it in our own persons; and we all stand justly
condemned for it.

Hence, also, he tells us that "by the offence of one,
judgment came upon all men to condemnation."
Besides, we have all contracted a vast debt upon ourselves and lie under much actual guilt, and that of a
scarlet dye and crimson tincture. Alas, we have done
little *but* sinned ever since we came into the world.
And, indeed, as long as we are out of Christ, either all
we do is sin, or at least we sin in all we do. We are every
day running up new scores, adding sin to sin and guilt
to guilt. And O how great, then, must our debts to law

and justice be? You look upon that man to be deeply in debt, indeed, whose debts are so many and great that he can neither know nor count them. And thus it is with us; so many and so great are our sins and, consequently, our debts to law and justice that we can neither know nor count them.

David, though a holy man, cried out, "Who can understand his errors?" Alas, who of us can count the sins of one day? They pass our knowledge and, which is worse still, we are under a necessity, while in our natural state, of increasing our sin and guilt every day and hour. Now, how shall this debt be paid, this sin and guilt be expiated and done away? Why, only by Christ. Close with Him in a marriage covenant and your souls are discharged from all. Justice, that stands upon satisfaction, calls for full payment. Its language is, "Pay or perish; pay or be damned." And we have nothing of our own to pay the least of all our debts; nor can we possibly right God for the wrong we have done Him by the least sin; and, which adds to our misery, we are every day in danger of arrests, nor know we how soon justice will, by the hand of that grim sergeant, death, clap an arrest upon us and cast us into prison, whence there is no redemption until we have paid the utmost farthing, which can never be.

Now, sinner, would you have your debts paid, your sins pardoned, and your soul freed from the danger of those arrests? Then give up yourself to Christ in a marriage covenant. O, this is the only way to discharge all! Christ says to justice concerning all His spouses, as Paul sometimes did to Philemon concerning Onesimus, "If he hath wronged thee, or oweth thee anything, put that upon my account." So says Christ to God concerning you, immediately upon your closing with Him: "Father, if this soul hath wronged Thee, and oweth Thee anything, place it on My account. I have taken all his debts upon Me. I will be responsible to Thee for all. Father, this soul I bled and died for; this soul I was made sin and a curse for, whereby Thy justice is fully satisfied. Let him, therefore, be discharged."

O soul, how should this draw you to Christ! Can you be content to lie under so great a debt? And is it a small thing to you to be in danger of so terrible an arrest as that of justice is, of which we have spoken? Suppose a man owed ten thousand pounds and had nothing wherewith to pay, and he saw himself in danger every moment of being cast into prison. How sad would you look upon his case to be. And how gladly, do you think, would he embrace an offer from any to discharge him from all? Soul, your case is ten thousand times more sad; and how gladly should you embrace the Lord Jesus, who would, and who alone can, discharge all for you! In short, we read of "spirits already in prison." Justice has already clapped its arrest upon thousands and ten thousands, and lodged them in the prison of eternal darkness; and what can you expect from it but to be dealt with in like manner speedily unless you close with Christ as your righteousness, to make satisfaction for you? His righteousness is such as makes a full satisfaction, and is every way answerable to the strictest demands of law and justice; and, by it, He being closed with by you, all your debts are paid at once.

2. *He supplies all their wants and makes blessed provision for them.* It is the part of a husband to supply the wants

of his wife, and to make provision for her; and this Christ does for all His spouses. He supplies all their needs according to His riches in glory. They have wants and He has fullness; they have needs and He has riches; and He brings His fullness to their wants and freely communicates the one to the other. Truly, we are full of wants of all sorts, wants in the soul and wants in the body. We are poor, miserable, blind, and naked; yea, our wants are such, and so pinching upon us, that, with the prodigal, we are even perishing with hunger. Even the saints themselves are a poor and needy people, full of wants. Now, how shall these wants be supplied? Only by Christ; and do but close with Him and He will supply all plentifully. Let it be but a day of espousals between Christ and you, and all your wants are supplied forever.

The truth is, Christ is all. He is the great all, as one calls Him; heaven and earth, time and eternity, grace and glory, are all in one Christ. He supplies the spiritual wants of His spouses. Do you want life? "He that hath the Son hath life." Do you want grace? Close with Christ and He will give you grace, abundance of grace. Do you want peace? Close with Christ, and He will give you peace. Do you want strength and righteousness—righteousness for justification, and strength for sanctification and obedience? Close with Christ and He will supply you with abundance of both. Do you want joy and consolation? Close with Christ. He will in due season fill you with joy and consolation. He will comfort your hearts. He supplies all the outward wants also of His spouses; and that so as they want no good thing. They want no outward good thing, but what they want thereof is better than the enjoyment of it would be.

True, they may, and often have, but a little of outward comforts; but yet then they have much in a little: much love, much blessing, much of Christ and the covenant; and therefore, a little which they have is said to be better than the riches of the many wicked. Besides, wherein they are cut short in temporals, Christ often makes it up to them in spirituals. They are poor in this world, but rich in faith. They have not much of the streams, it may be, but they have more of the fountain; more love and a sweeter communion with Christ. In a word, whatever heaven or earth affords, so far as they need it, they shall have it. "The Lord will give grace and glory, and no good thing will He withhold from them that walk uprightly." O who would not close with this Christ? Soul, why do you stand off from Him? Is there any who can supply your wants but He? Is there any who can give you life, peace, pardon, righteousness, and salvation but He? Or would you rather die in your wants than come to this fountain to be supplied? Would you rather perish in your own poverty than come to this treasury to be enriched?

3. *He heals all their wounds and cures all their maladies.* He is a physician to His spouses; and a physician such that, though the wound is never so deep and the disease never so desperate, yet He never fails to work the cure for them. O how should this allure us to Him! We, my beloved, have our wounds as well as our wants. We are full of maladies and diseases of soul. The truth is, from the sole of the foot to the crown of the head there is no soundness in us. The saints themselves have their wounds; yea, wounds many times that stink, and are corrupt. Indeed, they are apt to get fresh wounds

every day—wounds in their grace and wounds in their peace, wounds in their comforts and wounds in their consciences, wounds that smart sorely and which, many times, bleed, as if they should bleed to death of them. Well, but Christ heals all their wounds; and do but close with Him in a marriage covenant and He will heal all yours too, whoever you are. He is that good Samaritan who has oil and wine, His blood and Spirit, to pour into the wounds of His people for healing them; by His stripes we are healed. His blood and Spirit are a sovereign balm which can heal the deepest wounds and deadliest diseases. His spouses find it so; "He restoreth my soul," says David. His soul was subject to many ails and infirmities, but Christ restored him under all. Need we say, "Is there no balm in Gilead? Is there no physician there?" Surely there is. Indeed, there is none but Christ and His blood that can heal our wounds. O soul, why should you not close with Him that you may be healed? Do not your wounds stink? And are they not ready to rankle and gangrene? And, unless Christ heals them for you, must you not unavoidably die of them and perish forever? Must you not suffer a cutting off; a cutting off from God, a cutting off from Christ, a cutting off from heaven and all happiness forever? And will you suffer such a cutting off? Will you be content to die and perish eternally rather than come to Christ for healing?

4. *He bears all their burdens.* We are commanded to bear one another's burdens. Especially husbands should bear the burdens of their wives. And this Christ does; He bears all the burdens of His spouses. Sirs, we all have our burdens which we labor under; burdens

within and burdens without; burdens in the flesh and
burdens in the spirit; burdens that make us groan under them. "Being burdened we groan," says the Apostle. Burdens that are too heavy for us to bear, as David
complained his were; burdens sometimes that make us
a burden to ourselves, as Job complains of himself; yea,
burdens that make our very lives a burden to us. "My
soul is weary of my life," says Job.

Now, how shall all these burdens be borne? Why,
Christ will bear them all. He bears all the burdens of
all His spouses; and, if we will close with Him in a marriage covenant, there shall not that burden lie upon us
that He will not bear for us.

How Christ Bears His People's Burdens

He bears all His people's burdens two ways:

First, in a way of sympathy and compassion. He
weeps with all their tears and sighs with all their
groans. If they are troubled, He grieves; if they are
wounded, He bleeds. In all things, He bears the other
end of the burden. "In all their afflictions He was afflicted." He suffers together with us, or, as the Apostle
renders it, "He is touched with the feeling of our infirmities." He is deeply sensible of our burdens, of all
our sorrows. Such, sometimes, is the case with the
saints that, among men, they have none to pity and
sympathize with them under their burdens, as was
David's case, Psalm 69. But even then Christ bears the
other end of the burden. He pities them and sympa-
thizes with them, and that according to the weight of
their burdens. And O how sweet is that! "No matter,"
says a holy man, "how heavy the burden is, so long as

Christ bears the other end of it."

Second, in a way of succor and corroboration. He not only bears with them, but also gives them strength to bear and stand up under the burden. He puts His everlasting arms underneath him. And, with the promise of this, He encourages them to cast their burdens upon Him. "Cast thy burden upon the Lord, and He shall sustain thee," succor and support you. He strengthens and succors them, and that answerable to the weight of their burden. He gives them great strength for great burdens, great succors for great temptations; and so makes good His promise to them not to suffer them to be tempted above what they are able to bear.

The poor soul many times cries out, "O, I shall sink under the burden, it is too heavy for me to bear." But soul, though it is too heavy for you, yet it is not too heavy for Christ to bear; and He bears with you and for you; yea, He not only bears, but in due time He bears away all their burdens for them. There is not that burden lying upon any of His spouses but He so bears it as, at last, to bear it utterly away for them so as they shall never need to groan under it more. He has already borne the heaviest burden of all for them, even the guilt and punishment of their sins. "He bare our sins in His body on the tree"; and again, "He bare the sin of many." And it is well for us that He has borne this burden, for, otherwise, it must necessarily have sunk and crushed us forever. We could never have stood under it; and, as He has borne this, so He bears and, in due time, will bear away all for them. Are their sins, the iniquities of their holy things a burden to them? These He bears away from them. Are the re-

mainders of original corruption a burden to them?
These lie heavy upon some; in due time He bears these
away also; He turns their conflicts into triumphs. O
how should this comfort the heart of saints! And how
should it draw and allure sinners to Him! O, sirs, will
you sink under your burdens rather than have Christ
to bear them for you? O be not so cruel to your own
souls!

5. *He sweetens all their afflictions for them.* Afflictions
they may, and often do, meet with, many and great afflictions. Christ tells us that in the world we shall have
tribulation, but He sweetens all for them. He turns
their wormwood into wine; and, therefore, at the same
time, with the same breath, He says, "In me you shall
have peace." As if He should say, "I will sweeten all
your tribulations to you."

How Christ Sweetens His People's Afflictions

Christ sweetens His people's afflictions to them two
ways:
First, by His presence with them, and the commu-
nications of His love to them, under their afflictions.
Christ has promised to be with His people and to comfort them in their afflictions, Isaiah 43:2, "When thou
passest through the waters, I will be with thee; and
through the fire, it shall not burn thee"; that is, I will
be with you in all the sharpest afflictions you meet
with. They meet with many afflictions: sickness,
poverty, reproach, persecution, and the like; but Christ
is with them in all and shows them His love, and this
sweetens all to them. The truth is, Christ is never more

with His people, and He never communicates more of His love and consolations to them, than when they are in affliction. Then usually it is that they have the sweetest embraces of His bosom; then they have the clearest sights, the fullest tastes, the choicest and most eminent sealings of His love to them. Then he leads them into His banqueting house and displays the banner of His love over them. He stays them with flagons and comforts them with apples; His left hand is under their head and His right hand embraces them. Then He ministers His strongest consolations to them, comforting them in all their tribulations. The truth is, their sharpest afflictions are but to prepare them for His sweetest consolations; and, indeed, He therefore oftentimes afflicts them, that He may manifest His love and minister consolations to them, according to Hosea 2:14, "I will allure her into the wilderness and speak comfortably to her." And, indeed, as strong consolations oftentimes prepare for great afflictions, so great afflictions usually make way for strong consolations. "Affliction," said a worthy divine, "is the air in which Christ's love especially breathes; and Christ and the cross are sweet company."

Christ's love and presence with His people in their affliction is what turns their night into day, their darkness into light, their pains into ease, their sorrows into joy, their losses into gain, yea, and death itself into life. "Though I walk through the valley of the shadow of death, will I yet fear no evil, for Thou art with me," Psalm 23:4. It turns a prison into a pleasant palace; yea, it turns a fiery furnace into a beautiful walk, as in the case of the three children; and this experienced souls find. O how sweet are the afflictions when Christ and

His love come with them!

Second, by sanctifying their afflictions to them and working good to their souls out of all. Sanctified afflictions are sweet afflictions. They meet with afflictions, but Christ gives them the sweet fruit, and a blessed issue of them makes them all work together for good to them, according to that great oracle, Romans 8:28, "All things shall work together for good to them that love God." By these He proves their graces and improves their experiences. He makes them all to be, as the Gibeonites sometimes were to the congregation of God, as so many hewers of wood and drawers of water to their faith, to their comforts, to their holiness on earth, and happiness in heaven. The faith of this sweetened Job's great and heavy afflictions to him. "When I am tried," says he, "I shall come forth as gold." Hereby He tries their faith, which is better than gold. Hereby He refines them and purges away their dross from them. "Behold, I have refined thee, but not with silver; I have chosen thee in the furnace of affliction." Hereby He makes them partakers of His holiness. "By this He purgeth away their iniquity, and taketh away their sin."

In short, hereby He humbles them and seals instruction to them. Hereby He weans them from the world, draws them nearer to Himself, quickens their hearts in His good ways, and raises them up to highest strains of grace and pitches in holiness than they were got up to before; yea, hereby He increases their revenue of glory, and adds to their crown in eternity. "Our light afflictions, which are but for a moment," says the Apostle, "work out for us a far more exceeding and eternal weight of glory."

Thus He sanctifies all, and O how does this sweeten all! "Here is a cross, it is true," may the soul say, "but by this cross Christ crucifies me to sin and the world; He weans me from the creature, sets me longing after heaven; and so long welcome cross, however heavy. Here is an affliction, it is true, and it is a heavy one; but by it Christ proves and brightens my graces, and that sweetens all."

"O what owe I," said Rutherford, "to the file and hammer of my sweet Lord Jesus? He has taught me more by my six months' imprisonment than ever I learned before in my nine years' past ministry."

Luther was wont to say, "Three things make a good minister: temptation, affliction, and supplication." The same also conduce much to the making of a good Christian. And, indeed, it is seldom that ever a soul comes to any eminency in grace until he has been exercised with sanctified afflictions and temptations. And, doubtless, there is many a soul who may and must say that, next to Christ, His afflictions have, through His grace and blessing, been His best mercies. O how should this draw souls to Christ, and allure them into a marriage covenant with Him! Poor soul, it may be that which keeps you from Christ is the fear of what afflictions you may meet with in His ways. But know, first, you mayest meet with afflictions first or last, though you never close with Christ. For wicked men and unbelievers meet with troubles and afflictions, and that even in this world oftentimes. However, to be sure, at last they will have a full cup, yea, the very dregs of God's wrath poured out unto them. They will meet with and fall under sorer and more dreadful afflictions than any you can meet with in the way, and for the sake of

Christ. For, I pray consider, is there any trouble, any affliction, you can meet with for Christ like this, for a man to die in his sins, to be separated from God forever, to have infiniteness and eternity combined against you? Is there any trouble or affliction like the torments of the infernal pit and being the object of infinite wrath forever? And yet, this will be the lot at last of all that close not with Christ in marriage relation. Second, whatever afflictions you may meet with in the way of Christ, closing with Him sweetens all for you; and that so as that you would not have been without them for a world. O scare not at the cross, but close in with Christ!

6. *He subdues all their enemies for them.* True, the poor saints and spouses of Christ are beset with enemies on all hands; they have many enemies and mighty enemies; enemies within and enemies without, and all in confederacy against them to destroy them—to destroy their lives, to destroy their graces, to destroy their peace and comforts, to destroy their souls and happiness forever—all like so many roaring lions seeking to devour them. Well, but Christ, who is their Captain as well as their Husband, subdues and conquers all for them; and, first or last, makes them to set their feet upon necks and triumph over them. He makes them conquerors, yea, more than conquerors over all. He makes them so to conquer them as, sooner or later, to gain by all their conflicts and oppositions. Indeed, Christ has already conquered all His people's enemies for them. The saints have five great enemies: sin, self, the world, the devil, and death. Christ has long since conquered them all for them and, by degrees, brings

them into the joyful triumph of that conquest.

Christ has Conquered our Five Great Enemies

1. He has conquered sin for us. He, by being made sin, has obtained an eternal victory over sin for all His people. Sin is the saints' great enemy. It is that which wars against their souls. And, indeed, this is that which gives all the rest an advantage against them; but even this greatest enemy Christ has conquered for them. Hence, He is said to have condemned sin in the flesh. "He for sin hath condemned sin in the flesh." He, by being made a sacrifice for sin, has killed and subdued sin, passed a sentence of death and condemnation upon sin forever. Hence, also, our old man is said to be crucified with Him that the body of sin might be destroyed. Hence also He is said to destroy sin, to take away sin, and the like. And how? Why, as to the reign and power as well as the guilt and curse of it. And this Paul, acted upon by the spirit of faith, could triumph in, even while he was in the sharpest conflicts with sin. "I thank God through Christ," says he. For what? Why, for victory over, and deliverance from, the law of sin he was now conflicting with.

2. He has conquered self for us. Self, as well as sin, is our deadly enemy. This, indeed, is a near, close enemy, and most difficult to be slain. This is an enemy that we are too loath, many times, to have destroyed, and yet an enemy which makes woeful spoil upon us and our happiness. I often think of the speech of a holy and learned divine, "O, if I could be master of that house idol, my self, my own, my own will, wit, credit, and ease, how blessed were I! O but we have

need to be redeemed from ourselves, rather than from the devil and the world!" And immediately again he cries out, "O wretched idol, myself! when shall I see thee wholly decourted, and Christ wholly put in thy room!" And who that have any acquaintance with themselves do not find cause to cry out in like manner, "O this self, this wretched self, how great an enemy is it?" Well, but this Christ has conquered; and, closing with Him, you shall by degrees find it to die, and fall under you. Paul did so. "I am crucified with Christ," said he, "nevertheless I live; yet not I." He had an I, a self, which ruled in him. But by Christ it was crucified and slain for him, and he was a conqueror over it.

3. He has conquered the world for us. Take the world in what notion you will and it is, in one respect or another, an enemy to the saints. The men of the world, the things of the world, the frowns of the world, the flatteries of the world all, one way or other, fight against them and are enemies to them. The world, as well as sin and self, is a mortal enemy to them; but this enemy also Christ has subdued and conquered for them. He has told them so much for their comfort under the oppositions they meet with from it, John 16:33, "Be of good cheer, I have overcome the world." Says Christ, "The world is your enemy, but it is a conquered enemy. It will molest and oppose you, but it shall not be able to hurt you, for I have conquered it for you." And, as He has conquered it for us, so He will enable us, closing with Him by faith, to conquer it. So 1 John 5:4, "This is the victory which overcometh the world, even our faith." The world shall not always annoy and infest the saints.

4. He has conquered the devil, yea, all the devils in

hell for us. The devil is the enemy of the saints and, indeed, he is a formidable one; an adversary that "goeth about as a roaring lion, seeking whom he may devour." He is a subtle, a potent, a malicious, a cruel, and an indefatigable enemy. But so formidable an enemy as he is, Christ has conquered him for them. Hence He is said to have destroyed the devil. "He partook of flesh and blood, that through death He might destroy him that had the power of death; that is, the devil. And He is said to have "spoiled principalities and powers; and to have made a show of them openly on His cross, triumphing over them"; dragging them at His chariot wheels, as was the manner sometimes for conquerors to deal with their vanquished enemies. The sum is that He has made a complete and glorious conquest over all the devils in hell for believers. He has conquered them even to triumph. Christ has conquered the devil for His spouses, as to his ruling, reigning, and commanding power, and He will and does conquer him at last; yea, speedily, as to his tempting, vexing, and seducing power. "The God of peace shall tread Satan under your feet shortly." Shortly, soul, the devil shall vex you no more, molest you no more, infest and annoy you by his temptations no more.

5. He has conquered death for them. Death is an enemy, and it is the last enemy that is to be destroyed; and in itself considered, it is a terrible enemy; it is the king of terrors. But this enemy Christ has conquered for all His; He has taken away all its killing power, its sting and curse, insomuch that they may holily triumph over it and rejoice in its approach. The Apostle did so; "Death," says he, "is swallowed up in victory; O death, where is thy sting? O grave, where is thy victory? The

sting of death is sin, the strength of sin is the law; but
thanks be to God who giveth us the victory through
our Lord Jesus Christ." O what a triumph does He here
act over death through the conquest Christ has gotten
over it for him! Truly, this enemy is so far conquered
by Him for them that it is become indeed a friend to
them; and they can, when in a right spirit, embrace it
and long for it as such. Christ, by death, has unstung
death, and, in a sort, "undeaths" it. Thus Christ has
conquered all His people's enemies. And they, being
made one with Him in a marriage covenant, all His vic-
tories are theirs, and His conquests theirs, and they are
conquerors over all in Him. And O how sweet, how en-
couraging is this! And how should it win souls to close
with Him! Poor soul, you see yourself environed with
enemies; you are beset on all hands; legions of lusts
and devils attend with self; death and the world oppose
themselves against you. And you are often crying out,
as David in another case, "I am weak, and these men,
the sons of Zeruiah, are too strong for me," yea, you
are ready to say of them, as he sometimes in his unbelief did of Saul, "I shall one day perish by the hand of
Saul. Alas, I am a weak, nothing creature, and am un-
able to grapple with the least of all my enemies, and
how then shall I stand up against them all? Surely, I
shall perish by them at last."

Well, soul, know for your encouragement that all
you enemies are conquered by Christ. And though
they are too strong for you, yet they are not too strong
for Christ to grapple with and make you a conqueror
over. When the Prophet's servant saw what a great and
formidable host encompassed the city, he cried out,
"Alas, master, what shall we do?" And what did his mas-

ter answer him? "Fear not," said he, "for they that are
with us are more than they that are with them." So,
poor soul, when you consider what great and formidable enemies compass you about, you cry out to
one and another, "Alas, sir, what shall I do?" But I
would say to you, as the Prophet to his servant, "Fear
not, there is more with you than with them. You have
Christ with you to fight and overcome all for you;
therefore, cheer up! Give up yourself unto Him, and
the victory over sin, self, world, death, devil, and all is
yours forever. O, who would not have such a husband!

7. *He minds and manages all their concerns for them.* It
is the part of a husband to mind and manage the concerns of his wife, and to have a natural care both of her
and them. And thus it is with Christ. He manages all
His people's concerns, and that in heaven, on earth,
and in our own souls.

He minds and manages all their concerns in
heaven for them. Their affairs lie much in heaven;
their business there is great. And Christ their Husband
minds all and transacts all for them, and that faithfully.
Indeed, He went there on purpose to transact their affairs for them. Hence He is said to have "entered not
into the holy place made with hands, but into heaven
itself, there to appear in the presence of God for
them." Hence also He is said to be an Advocate with
the Father for them. He pleads with the Father for
them. Have they a petition to present to the Father for
this or the other mercy? He presents and offers it for
them; He takes all their prayers and sprinkles them
with His own blood, perfumes them with the odors of
His own incense, and then offers them to the Father

with His own hand. We pray very brokenly, but He
mends our prayers; yea, oftentimes, when we cannot
pray, when we cannot speak for ourselves, He speaks
for us and offers our petitions for us. Are their charges
and accusations brought in against them, either by
Satan, the accuser of the brethren, on the one hand,
or by the law and justice of God, which are daily
wronged and violated, on the other hand? Why, Christ
interposes for them. He answers and invalidates all. He
rebukes Satan. In the first place we find Joshua standing before the angel of the Lord, and Satan standing at
His right hand to resist (or accuse) Him. And we have
Christ sharply rebuking Satan for this accusation. "The
Lord said unto Satan, the Lord rebuke thee, O Satan;
even the Lord that hath chosen Jerusalem, rebuke
thee." And, as He rebukes Satan, so He satisfies the law
and justice of His Father. Hence He is said to make intercession for them; and that to the overthrowing of all
those counter pleas which law or justice can put
against them. Have they sinned and need a new pardon, need to have things set right between God and
them afresh? This also Christ does for them. "If any
man sin, we have an advocate with the Father, Christ
Jesus the righteous, and He is the propitiation for our
sins." While they, through weakness and temptation,
are sinning on earth, He, out of His grace and love, is
pleading with the Father for them in heaven. Thus He
minds all their concerns in heaven for them.
      He minds and manages all their concerns on earth
for them. The saints have their affairs and concerns on
earth among men, as well as in heaven with the Father;
and Christ, their Husband, minds and transacts all
these likewise for them. Indeed, He is ever mindful of

them, to do them good and to promote their interest. Hence, says He, "the Father worketh hitherto, and I work. I am always at work for your good." Are they wronged and oppressed by enemies? He avenges all their wrongs. Hence He is said to reprove kings for their sakes, and, elsewhere, to plead their cause against their enemies and the like. Do they need deliverance and salvation out of trouble and distresses? He brings salvation to them. Do they need conduct and guidance through their difficulties and temptations in the wilderness of the world? He leads and guides them. "He leads Joseph like a flock"; and elsewhere, "I will guide thee with Mine eye." He carries them through all their straits and difficulties; and even when He seems most to forget them, even then He is ever mindful of them and their concerns, for He has graven them upon the palms of His hands and their walls are continually before Him. And, though they often say, "The Lord has forsaken me, and my God has forgotten me," yet He never forsakes or forgets them, nor can He. No, a woman may sooner forget her sucking child and not have compassion upon the son of her womb than He can forget His people.

He minds and manages all their concerns for them in their own souls. The saints have many great concerns to be minded within them, concerns of great moment and importance, and, were they to be minded and managed only by themselves, they would make but poor work. O! but Christ their Husband minds and manages all these likewise for them; and, to be sure, they cannot miscarry in His hand. He gives them His Spirit to work all their works in them and for them. He observes what grace, what strength, what counsel, what comfort, they stand in need of, and, by His Spirit, ministers all to them. Hence He is said to give them grace and mercy in time of need, seasonable supplies; and to be both the author and finisher of their faith. He minds and observes how the great work goes on in their souls, and He takes care for the prospering and perfecting of it. O how should this draw us to Christ and encourage us to accept of the offers of His love!

8. *He joins them in eternal life and glory.* Husbands used to make their wives joint possessors; they entitle them to such or such lands and inheritances. So Christ joins all His spouses in no less than eternal life and blessedness. He makes over a great jointure to them; glory, a weight of glory, an eternal and exceeding weight of glory; an inheritance in light, an inheritance incorruptible undefiled, and "that fadeth not away"; a kingdom, an everlasting kingdom, an everlasting kingdom prepared for them before the foundation of the world; a crown of life; a crown of righteousness; a crown of glory which never fades and never withers. The truth is, He endows them with all His treasures, riches, and dignities, with all the privileges of His house, with all the purchase of His blood, with all the blessings of His love, with all the treasures of heaven, with all the glories of eternity.

Behold, whatever is in the promise, whatever is in the covenant, whatever is in the glorious counsel of election, whatever the heart of God could give, the wisdom of God contrive, the power of God produce, or the blood of God purchase, that, all that, Christ jointures His people in. O sirs, how should this draw and allure us to Christ! Is heaven and eternal life worth nothing? Are all the glories of eternity of no value? O, who are you that Christ should be willing to enstate you into all this? In yourselves, you are lying in the lap and bosom of hell, heirs of wrath and condemnation, in danger every moment of sinking into the infernal pit. But lo! Christ comes and makes love to you; and, if you accept Him, He will entitle you unto life and blessedness, to such things as "eye hath not seen, nor ear heard, nor hath it entered into the heart of man to conceive of." Take Him, therefore, I beseech you, in your most intimate embraces.

Thus you see, in part, what great things Christ does for His spouses. Now, will you accept Him or will you not? May I not say to you, as Saul sometimes did to His servants, "Hear, now, will the son of Jesse give to every one of you fields, and vineyards, and make you captains of thousands?" So, will sin or the world or the laws to which you are naturally wedded do such great things for you as Christ will? Will these pay your debts for you, supply your wants for you, or heal your wounds for you? Will these secure your eternal interest for you and make you happy in the other world as Christ would? Alas! they can do none of all this. O close, close therefore with Christ, who can and will do all!

Chapter 9

Which opens a little the heart of Christ, and shows how much He is set upon an espousal to sinners

Surely Christ is the best Husband, and none can do such great things as He for his spouses, which renders an espousal to Him very desirable. But will He take such as we are into so near a relation with Him? Has He any mind, any heart, to the business? Any mind, any heart! His heart is set upon nothing more than an espousal with sinners coming to Him, and His soul longs after them. Never did the most passionate lover more long for an espousal between him and his beloved than Christ does for an espousal between Himself and sinners. And because love is the loadstone of love, and the most powerful attraction, in order to the more effectual drawing and alluring your souls to Christ, I shall a little, in a few particulars, open my sweet Lord's heart to you in this business. And O that the reports of His love to you, and His willingness to espouse you to Himself, might draw your Hearts out a little in love to Him, and work you into a willingness to be espoused!

1. *Such is the heart of Christ, and so set upon an espousal with sinners, that He willingly became incarnate, bled and died in order hereunto; and O how should this draw us to Him!* Should you see a man do some great act of self-denial and abasement and, withal, freely venture his

life in order to his obtaining such or such a one for his
wife, you would easily conclude that his heart was
much set upon an espousal with her. Lo, then! Christ
has greatly denied and abased Himself. He became incarnate, and not only freely ventured but laid down
His life in order to an espousal between Himself and
sinners. And how much, then, must His heart be in the
business?

1.) He became incarnate in order hereunto.
Had not Christ been incarnate, we would never possibly have been espoused unto Him, nor have enjoyed
conjugal communion with Him; but that we might be
capable of and arrive unto such a happiness, He who
in Himself was the eternal Son freely became incarnate, assumed human nature into union with His divine person. Hence it is said, "The Word became
flesh." Not that there was a transmutation of God into
flesh; but the Word of God, that is, God the Son, the
second Person in the Trinity, assumed flesh, human
nature, into union with Himself; and so near is that
union into which the human nature is assumed with
the person of the Son of God that that nature has no
subsistence but what it has in His divine Person. And
for that end, among others, as a learned divine has observed, it is so expressed, "The Word was made flesh;
namely, to note the infinite nearness of that union
which our nature is taken into with the divine person;
it being so near, as that it has no subsistence of its own,
but is, as it were, wholly melted into the personality of
the Son of God." Hence also He is said to partake of
flesh and blood, to be manifested in the flesh and the
like. And O what an act of self-denial and abasement
was this! And how great was Christ's condescension

herein! In Philippians 2:6-7, the Apostle speaks of it as the greatest abasement He could stoop unto: "Who (speaking of Christ) being in the form of God, thought it not robbery to be equal with God; but made himself of no reputation, and took upon Him the form of a servant, and was made in the likeness of men." Pray, mark it. He was in the form of God, that is, He was as truly and really God as the Father was and He thought it no robbery to be equal with God. That is, He had all those divine excellencies and perfections in Him which the Father had in Him, and yet He took upon Him the form of a servant, and was made in the likeness of men; that is, He became incarnate. He became man.

Well, what does this argue? Even infinite condescension. Therefore, he tells us that herein He became of no reputation, or, as the Greek is, He emptied Himself of His glory. His glory was veiled and clouded hereby. The glory of His Godhead was eclipsed. It is true, indeed, His Godhead was not hereby lost or laid aside. No, He was as much and truly God after His incarnation as He was before. He did not cease to be God by becoming man, but, as one of the ancients expresses it, "He was made that which He was not, and yet remained that which He was." He was made man, yet so as that He still remained to be God. But though his Godhead was not lost or laid aside hereby, yet hereby was the glory of it veiled and lost for a time, and He was content to have it so. O how great a condescension was this! O! for Him who was God, God equal with the Father, to become man, to cover Himself with the coarse veil of our flesh and be content for so long a time to lose the glory of His deity, which was infinitely dear to Him, and all this to make way for an espousal between Himself and poor sinners. What self-abasement was this! And how should it encourage souls to look after an espousal to Him.

2.) He not only became incarnate, but also freely bled and died in order hereunto; which is a further discovery of his heart herein. "Being found in fashion as a man, He humbled himself, and became obedient unto death, even the death of the cross"; that is, to the most formidable death, a death of pain, a death of shame, an accursed death. Hence also it is said that "He gave Himself an offering and a sacrifice unto God for us." Yea, not only did He bleed, suffer, and die, but He did all freely, and with much readiness and enlargedness of soul. Hence He is said to have "poured out his soul unto death." He seemed in a holy manner prodigal of His life in the case; He thought neither blood, nor life, nor anything too much for them. O, how much does this argue His heart to be upon the business! It spoke much of Jacob's heart to be so much set upon having Rachel for his wife that He could be content to undergo as much hard service for her as he did, even seven years' service. Jacob, it is said, served seven years for Rachel, yea, and they seemed to him but a few days for the love he had to her. So surely it argues Christ's heart to be much set upon an espousal with sinners, that He was content not only to serve, but even bleed and die for them in order hereunto. O, sirs, behold and wonder! Christ comes from heaven, quits His throne, leaves the bosom of His Father in which He had, with infinite delight, lain from eternity! Behold and wonder, the Lord of life dies. The God of blessing was made a curse, the infinitely beloved Son treads the winepress of the Father's wrath;

heaven descends into hell, glory veils and eclipses itself under shame and ignorance. The infinitely holy One is made sin, and all this to redeem, and redeeming, espouse poor sinners to Himself! And is not His heart upon the business, do you think? And has He not love for them? O be not faithless but believe.

2. *Such is the heart of Christ, and so set upon an espousal with sinners, that He condescends sweetly to woo them, and solicits them for their love and acceptance of Him.* Should you see a man with all earnestness and importunity wooing a virgin, making love to her, following her from day to day with renewed offers and solicitations, you would conclude his heart was much set upon an espousal with her. And is it not thus with the Lord Jesus towards poor sinners? Does he not woo them, and make love to them, and that with all earnestness and pressing importunity, following them with renewed offers and solicitations from day to day? Now He meets them in this ordinance, and there He woos them and makes love to them; anon He meets them in that ordinance, and there woos them and makes love to them. Now He sends His ministers and, by them, woos them and makes love to them. Anon He sends His Spirit, and by it woos them and makes love to them. Thus He is every way, and upon all occasions, wooing them. And in his wooing of them how earnestly does He call and invite them to Himself! It is not a cold offer or a slight motion only that He makes to them, but He moves and offers, calls and invites, with all earnestness and importunity. "Ho! every one that thirsteth, come ye to the waters; come ye, yea, come." And again, "The spirit and the bride say come; and let

him that is athirst come."

How vigorously does He plead and expostulate the business with them! Christ not only calls and invites, but He also pleads and expostulates with sinners in the case, and that in the most winning way, and with the most weighty arguments that possibly may be. "Ho! every one that thirsteth, come unto the waters. Wherefore do ye spend your money for that which is not bread, and your labor for that which satisfieth not? Incline your ear, and come unto me. Hear, and your soul shall live; and I will make with you an everlasting covenant, even the sure mercies of David." And again, "Turn ye, turn ye, why will ye die, O house of Israel? I have no pleasure in your damnation but would rather that you would come unto Me and live. Why will you die? Is not life better than death? Is not heaven better that hell? Is not my love better than lust? Are not the pleasures of My presence, and at My right hand, which are forevermore, better than the pleasures of sin, which are but for a season, a short season? Why will you die? Is there no physician there? Am not I able to save you to the uttermost? And are not My arms wide open to receive you? Have not I died for that very end, that you might live? Look, here is My blood; here are my wounds; behold Me in the garden and see Me bleeding there for you. Behold Me upon the cross and see Me bleeding, yea, bleeding there to death for you. And then see if you can find in your heart to refuse Me any longer. In short, would you not lose all your cost and all your labor? Would you enjoy good, the best good, the most satisfying good? Have you any mind to life, and would you have your souls live forever? Have you any mind to My covenant and all the riches and treasures of that? Then accept Me and My love, in whom you shall have all."

How sweetly does He melt, and how tenderly does His heart yearn towards them and over them? He comes to them not only with invitations in His lips, but also with tears in His eyes and tender compassion in His heart strongly working towards them. Now He weeps and then He groans; now He drops a sigh and then a tear; and all to melt their hard and unbelieving hearts to draw and allure them to Himself. "O Jerusalem, Jerusalem," says He, "how often would I have gathered thee!" The repetition of the name shows the depth of His love and commiseration towards them. And indeed, I think I see how the tender heart of my dear Lord melts, and even bleeds, over this unbelieving city; and in them, all unbelieving sinners to whom He offers Himself. He is melted into tears towards them. So you have it, Luke 19:41-42. In Matthew He only groans, but in Luke He both weeps and groans. Lo, then! Here is sweet Jesus weeping and groaning; here is the joy of the whole earth, weeping and groaning, and that over Jerusalem, a bloody city; a city embroiled in the blood of His saints; and a city thirsty of His own blood, a city full of wickedness, full of the contempt of His gospel, His grace, His salvation.

How freely and openly He reveals and offers Himself to them. The offer Christ makes is not a limited offer, but general and extensive to all; nor is it an offer made upon hard and severe terms, but upon the terms of grace and love. "Look unto me and be saved, all ye ends of the earth. Ho! every one that thirsteth, come ye to the waters; and He that hath no money, come ye, buy and eat; yea, come, buy wine and milk,

without money, and without price. Come unto Me, all
ye that are weary, and heavy laden, and I will give you
rest. Whosoever is athirst, let him come unto me and
drink. Behold, I stand at the door and knock; if any
man will Hear my voice, and open the door, I will
come in." And again, "Whoever will, let him come and
take of the water of life freely." Mark it all: "Every one,
whoever will, though never so vile and sinful, never so
black and deformed, though he has been never so
desperate an enemy to Me and My glory. Surely, were
not His heart much in the business, He would not thus
freely and unlimitedly offer Himself.

How affectionately He beseeches and entreats
them. The tender, trembling child cannot more affectionately entreat and beseech his offended father to
spare him and be reconciled unto him than Christ entreats and beseeches offending sinners to be espoused
to Him, and be made happy by Him forever. "Now,
then we are ambassadors for Christ," says the Apostle,
"as though God did beseech you by us: we pray you in
Christ's stead, be ye reconciled to God," 2 Corinthians
5:20. Pray mark, here is praying and beseeching; the
Lord of glory, as it were, upon His knees to poor sinners, begging them to accept His love: "We pray you in
Christ's stead," that is, it is not we but Christ by us who
prays and beseeches you. O what condescension is this!

Once more, how sweetly does He draw and allure
them! "Draw me," says the spouse, "and we will run after thee." And indeed, He draws and allures souls, and
that with admirable sweetness. "I drew them with cords
of love, with the bands of a man." Now He sets His
beauty, riches, and glory before them, thereby to draw
and allure them. Anon He drops a little myrrh upon

the handle of the lock. He gives them some little taste and feeling of His grace and love thereby to draw and allure them. Now He sweetly insinuates His love to them; He tells them how much His heart is upon them, what great things He has done and suffered for them, and how He has no design upon them but to make them happy forever. Soon He lets them see how infinitely happy a marriage union and communion with Him would make them; He lets in some small glimpses of heaven and glory upon them; He opens the treasures of His covenant and kingdom to them; and all this to allure them to Himself. And over and above all this, He ever and anon comes and, as it were, takes the soul aside and, by the still voice of His Spirit, makes love to Him. "Come, poor soul," says He, "look upon thy bleeding, dying Savior; come, see what I have done, and what I have prepared for you. See what treasures of life and love, of grace and glory, there are in Me. Look, here is My love. Taste and see if it is not better than wine. Here is My bosom; make your bed in it, and see if it is not a warm bosom. Come, soul, though you have no love for Me, yet I have love for you, and would fain have you happy forever. Why, therefore, should you stand at such a distance from Me?"

Thus He sweetly woos and solicits them for their love and acceptance of Him. Now, soul, does He thus woo you, and will you refuse Him? If so, know that the time of love will not always last; yea, and the time will come when, though you call and cry, yet He will not hear. Let me, therefore, say to you, as Paul to his Corinthians, "Receive not the grace of God in vain; for behold, now is the accepted time, now is the day of salvation."

3. *Such is the heart of Christ, and so set upon an espousal with sinners, that He not only thus woos them, but also waits long upon them, often renews the offer of His love to them, and puts up with many horrid affronts and provocations at their hands, if at last He may prevail with them.* Suppose a man should not only make love to a person, but he should also wait long upon her in the offers of his love; and that though he meets with many affronts and unkindnesses from her. This, you would say, would argue his heart to be much set upon her. And is it not thus with Christ towards poor sinners? O how long does He wait upon them! How often does He renew the offers of His love to them! And what affronts, indignities, and unkindnesses does He bear with at their hands! "Behold, I stand at the door and knock," says He. Standing is a waiting posture. Christ does not give a call or a knock at the door of the sinner's heart and then leave. No, He stands knocking. He gives call after call and knock after knock, being ever ready to enter if the soul will at all open to Him. So again, "All the day long have I stretched forth My hands to a disobedient and gainsaying people; a people that provoketh Me to anger continually to My face." All the day long Christ waits, day after day, week after week, month after month, and year after year, upon sinners; yea, and many affronts and indignities He puts up with and passes by for them! "All the day long have I stretched forth My hands, opened the arms and bosom of my love, and that to a gainsaying and rebellious people; an opposing, refusing, resisting people; a people that provoked Me to My face continually every day; a people that are daily loading Me with their sins and provocations; a people that will not let Me go one day without

The Best Match

affronting Me, and that to My face; a people that are
every day daring Me to damn them." O, what patience
is this! So, Matthew 23:37, "O Jerusalem, Jerusalem,
how often would I have gathered thee, and thou
wouldst not?" How often! Not once, or twice, or ten
times, but very often. It notes that He waited long
upon them, and strove long with them, and that after
many and often repeated affronts and refusals on their
part, He still offered Himself and His love to them, and
thus He deals by sinners still. He offers Himself and
His love to them, but they will have none of Him; He
renews His offers and they renew their refusals; they
spurn His love, yet He makes love still, He tells them
what great preparations He has made, and how all
things are ready, and how welcome they shall be to the
marriage feast; but they make light of all, preferring a
worldly interest before Him and it.

Well, however, He leaves them not but sends again,
and calls again, notwithstanding all they do. In effect
they tell Him that they desire neither Him nor His
grace, that they would rather enjoy their lusts than His
love. They abuse His grace. They despise His correc-
tions. They slight His calls. They resist His Spirit. O
what affronts are these! And after all this, it may be, He
renews His suit, laying himself and His love at their
feet if yet He may win them to Himself. O how much
must His heart be upon an espousal with them! Soul,
let it melt you into love to Him. O who would with-
stand such a Lord, such a Lover! What? woo and wait
so long too? Put up with such and so many affronts and
still make love? Was there ever love and patience like
this?

4. *Such is the heart of Christ, and so set upon an espousal with sinners, that He has laid Himself under bonds to receive and accept them in case they are willing to be espoused to Him; and what greater discovery of His heart than this?* Should a young man lay himself under bonds to marry such and such a woman, though as yet she hated him, or was utterly averse to him, you would surely conclude that his heart was much set upon a match with her. And, truly, this is no more than Christ, the Lord of glory, has done. He is become bound to marry poor sinners to Himself; yea, though at present they hate Him and are altogether averse to Him. Yet in case they shall at last be willing to close with Him, He is become bound to receive them. He has become bound both to the Father and to them.

1.) He is bound to the Father to receive sinners, and espouse them to Himself, in case they come to Him. So much is held forth in John 6:27, "Labor not for the meat that perisheth, but for that meat which endureth unto everlasting life, which the Son of Man shall give unto you, for Him hath God the Father sealed"; that is, God the Father has ordained and appointed Christ. He has laid a law upon Him to give Him eternal life, and, therefore, Himself to sinners coming to Him. And we may, therefore, rest assured that He will do it. Yea, Christ looks upon Himself as under a law from the Father to do it, and therefore says, "Thy law is within My heart." His law, what law? Why, the law of His mediatorship, which commands Him as to die for sinners, so to accept sinners when they come unto Him. And surely He that so freely fulfilled it in the one will not be disobedient to it in the other. In a word, in that covenant, by divines called the

covenant of redemption, which passed between the
Father and Jesus Christ from eternity concerning the
salvation of sinners, Christ became bound to the
Father to receive all that should come to Him and He
will be faithful.

  2.) He is bound to sinners themselves in the
case. He has indeed given them His bond. He has
given them His promise which is His bond, and a
strong one too, an invincible obligation. And the soul
may look on it as such. But where is His promise?
Truly, the whole gospel is but, as it were, one general
promise made by Him to this purpose. But take one
for all the rest: John 6:37, "All that the Father giveth
Me shall come unto Me; and him that cometh unto Me
I will in no wise cast out." That is, "I will most assuredly
receive him, and bestow Myself eternal life upon him."
And how often has He renewed this bond of His! Yea,
and that it may be firm and valid to our faith, as well as
in itself, He has hereunto added His seal, and that
such a seal as renders it altogether unquestionable for
it is the seal of His own blood. Hence the gospel is
called the New Testament in His blood, that is, sealed
and ratified in his blood. And His blood is called the
blood of the covenant because the covenant and
promises thereof are sealed with that blood. Yea, more
yet—if His promise and seal are not enough, they shall
have more, for to both of these He has added His oath
for their further security in the case. "Verily, verily,"
says He, "He that believeth on Me hath everlasting life,
and shall not come into condemnation." And again,
"Verily, verily, the hour cometh, and now is, when the
dead shall hear the voice of the Son of God, and they
that hear shall live," John 5:25.

"As I live" was the form of God's oath in the Old Testament, and He there swears that He has no pleasure in the death of sinners but would rather they would turn and live. "Verily, verily" is the form of Christ's oath in the New Testament, and He there swears that souls shall live by coming to Him. "O happy we," as one of the ancients cries out, "for whose sakes God doth swear; but O unbelieving we, if we do not believe Him swearing."

Thus, Christ has given us His bond, His promise, and that sealed with His blood, and to all added His oath for the further encouragement of our faith. And what can we desire more? If you have a man's promise to you for the performance of this or that, you think you are well, judging him to be both able and faithful. But if you have his seal added to his promise, then you look upon yourselves secure of the business indeed. But if to both these you have his oath added, then you look on the business past all doubt and you dare not question it. Why, lo! Christ has given poor sinners all this to assure them that He will embrace and accept them coming to Him. And O how firm may their faith stand upon all this! And what horrid wickedness must it be to so much as once to question it! True, neither His seal, nor His oath, adds anything to the truth and certainty of the promise itself, but it adds to our sense and apprehension, and merely out of indulgence to us and our weakness are the one and the other added.

So the Apostle tells us, Hebrews 6:17-18, "God willing more abundantly to show to the heirs of promise the immutability of His counsel, confirmed it by an oath; that by two immutable things, wherein it was impossible for God to lie, we might have strong consolation, who have fled for refuge, to lay hold upon the hope set before us." Mark, it was not to confirm or add anything to the truth and certainty of God's counsel or covenant that His oath was added, but it was to confirm and encourage our faith. Thus you see Christ is under bonds to receive and accept sinners if they come to Him and are willing of an espousal with Him; and how much does this argue His heart to be in the business! O let none ever say, "Will Christ accept and receive me coming to Him?" For indeed, bonds bind Him so to do. The truth is, were He under no bonds, we need not question it; for His heart would constrain Him; and had He no heart, we need not doubt it, for bonds would bind Him to it. Christ must deny His Word, promise, seal, oath, and all, if He refuses any soul that indeed comes to Him and desires to close in a marriage covenant with Him. O what encouragement is this!

5. *Such is the heart of Christ, and so set upon an espousal with sinners, that He has given them a full and unquestionable assurance that nothing whatsoever shall stand between Him and them, nor prejudice their acceptance of Him, in case they are willing to be espoused unto Him.* Should a man not only make love to a person, wait long upon her in the offers thereof and the like, but also give a full assurance that nothing shall stand between him and her to hinder the match in case she is willing to accept him, this would argue his heart to be much upon her indeed. Now, this also Christ has done; He has given sinners a full and firm assurance that nothing shall prejudice their acceptance with Him, nor hinder the match between Him and their souls in case they are willing;

and is not His heart then much upon the business? This is no other than what He Himself declares, John 6:37; and certainly He does not delude souls with vain words. "Him that cometh unto Me," says He. That is, He who believes on Me, He who is willing to be Mine, "I will in no wise cast out." In no wise, or by no means, upon no account whatsoever; nothing shall obstruct his acceptance with Me, but I will receive him with it. Notwithstanding all his vileness, all his unworthiness, all his unkindness, all his unsuitableness, notwithstanding all that either men or devils, law or conscience, can charge upon him, yea, or that unbelief itself can pretend or allege, be it what it will, notwithstanding all, I will receive him into the bosom of My love.

Christ's language to poor sinners in this promise of His, and many more of like import, is such as this, "Come poor souls, be not afraid of Me, whatever your condition is, and however things stand and are stated with you, yet if you have a mind to Me, and an espousal with Me, assure yourselves that nothing shall obstruct your acceptance with Me. Nothing shall shut up My bosom against you, but I will betroth you to Myself forever." O what encouragement is here! Come to Christ and close with Him in a marriage covenant. "Who would not do that?" may some say. "But alas! there are a thousand things that will hinder the match, and stand between Him and me, should I go to Him." Poor soul! this is apparently the plea and language of unbelief, and let it be silenced forever, Christ having, as you see, fully assured us of the contrary. But besides, what is it that you fear or that any soul can fear will stand between Christ and you to hinder an espousal with Him? Bring forth your strong pleas and see if they will bear any weight in the sanctuary balance.

    1.) Is it outward meanness and baseness? Possibly you are low, mean, and base, in the world; you are a poor, forlorn, despicable creature, and this you think will stand between Christ and you. "Surely," you say, "Christ will never take such a contemptible worm as I am into such a relation with Himself." But, sinner, this shall not hinder in the least, for Christ is no respecter or persons. High and low, rich and poor, bond and free, are all one in Christ and to Christ; yea, does not the Word tell us that He chooses the poor of this world to be heirs of the kingdom and rich in faith? And again, "Ye see your calling, brethren," says the Apostle in 1 Corinthians 1:26, "how that not many wise men after the flesh, not many mighty, not many noble, are called, but God chooses foolish, and weak, and base ones." As greatness is no furtherance, so meanness and baseness is no hindrance in this case. Men indeed mind honor and greatness; they will have such as are suitable to themselves, but it is otherwise with Christ. Poor sinner, though you have been never so low, mean, and base in the world; though you should be clothed with rags; yet, if you have a mind to Christ, He will accept you and marry you to Himself; yea, and your soul will be as dear to Him, and as precious in His sight, as the soul of the greatest prince or monarch in the world.

    2.) Is it inward blackness and deformity? Perhaps, sinner, if you are not outwardly mean and base, yet you see yourself inwardly black and deformed, you lie in your blood and gore, wallowing in your sin and filth. Neither is there any worth and beauty in you for which Christ should desire you. And, therefore, you

say, "Surely Christ will have nothing to do with me, nor
so much as cast an eye or look of love upon me." But,
soul, this shall not stand between Christ and you either. But if you have a mind to Him, He will marry you
to Himself notwithstanding. For, indeed, Christ marries not any for their beauty, but those whom He marries He marries to make them beautiful. He mar-ries
them not for any worth of theirs but to put worth upon
them. And, indeed, there are none that He espouses to
Himself but He finds them black and deformed, in
their blood and gore, as well as you. And so they are till
He puts his beauty upon them. How sweet is that word,
Ezekiel 16:6-8, "When I passed by thee, and saw thee,
and saw thee polluted in thine own blood," that is, in
thy sin and filth, "I said unto thee, live; I said unto thee
when thou wast in thy blood, live; yea, when thou wast
in thy blood, live." Mark, three times He mentions it,
"in thy blood, in thy blood, in thy blood," to denote
the depth of that defilement we are under.

Well, and what then? Will Christ have anything to
do with such? Yes, He makes love to them. "Behold, thy
time was the time of love." He marries them to Himself
in an everlasting covenant. "I spread my skirt over thee,
and covered thy nakedness; yea, I swear unto thee, and
entered into covenant with thee, and thou becamest
Mine." Yea, not only so, but He puts a beauty, yea, His
own beauty and comeliness upon them. "Thou art
come to excellent ornaments, and art comely through
my comeliness which I have put upon thee." O soul, be
not discouraged, Christ will turn your blackness into
beauty, and will not cast you off because of it!

3.) Is it the greatness and heinousness of your
sin and guilt? "O my sins, my sins," says the poor soul,

"they are exceeding great. They are many and great in themselves and they are clothed with many and great aggravations. Few in the world ever sinned at that rate that I have done. Therefore I fear that Christ will never own me so as to take me into such a relation with Himself."

Well, be it so, yet know that this shall not stand between Christ and you, if you are willing to be espoused to Him. He has promised to pardon great sins, and to accept notwithstanding great sins, in case the soul is but willing. "Come now," says He, "and let us reason together; though your sins are as scarlet, they shall be as white as snow; though they are red like crimson, they shall be as wool." Though your sins are as scarlet and as crimson; that is, though they are great, foul, enormous sins, sins of a heinous and crying nature, and clothed with the greatest aggravations, yet they shall be white as snow and wool. That is, they shall be fully done away and pardoned as if they had never been so. Again, Isaiah 43:24-25; in the 24th verse He speaks to some who had made Him to serve with their sins, and wearied Him with their iniquities. These surely were great sinners, and their sins of a heinous crying nature; and yet, at the 25th verse, what a full promise of pardon does He make to them! "I, even I, am He that blotteth out thy transgressions for My own sake, and will not remember thy sins."

Poor soul, what shall I say? Have you abundantly sinned? Have you multiplied sins? He has promised abundantly to pardon, and to multiply pardons. Are you guilty of all manner of sins? And to your other sins have you added blasphemy? He has promised that "all manner of sin and blasphemy shall be forgiven, except

that against the Holy Ghost," which your complaining
of the greatness of your sins argues you are not guilty
of. O soul, be not discouraged because of the greatness
of your sins. Christ marries souls not because they are
not sinners, great sinners, but He marries them to take
away their sins, and to discharge them from them forever. And the greater your sins are, the greater will be
the glory of Christ's grace, which is what He aims at in
receiving you into so near and glorious a relation with
Himself as this is. Besides, what will you do with your
great sins unless you go with them to Christ? Great sins
argue a great need for Christ and call for great hastening unto Christ.

4.) Is it any former neglects or refusals of yours?
Possibly not only are your sins many and great, but
there is this added to all the rest: long and frequent refusals of Christ and His love. He has often called but
you have given Him no answer. He has long wooed you
but you have not complied with Him. O the many
sweet calls, gracious offers, loving offers, which He has
made to you and you have despised! And this makes
you fear that He will now have nothing to do with you.
And truly, soul, this is sad, very sad. Hereby Christ has
lost much glory which you might have brought Him;
hereby you have lost much sweet communion which
you might have enjoyed. Hereby Christ's heart has
been much grieved, which might have been prevented;
and hereby the work is made much more difficult than
at first it was, your heart being grown more hard, and
your corruptions more strong.

Thus it is every way very sad that you have thus neglected and refused Christ. But, yet, neither shall this
stand between Him and you, in case you are willing to

be espoused to Him. For this, see Proverbs 1:20-23, "Wisdom crieth without, she uttereth her voice in the streets; she crieth in the chief place of concourse, in the openings of the gates, in the city she uttereth her words, saying, How long, ye simple ones, will ye love simplicity, and scorners delight in their scorning, and fools hate knowledge? Turn ye at my reproof; behold, I will pour out My Spirit unto you, I will make known My words unto you." Pray observe, Christ has offered Himself and His love to them, but they had refused Him and it; yea, they had refused long, and refused with much contempt. "How long, ye simple ones, will ye love simplicity?" They scorned the offer of Christ and His love; and, yet, here He renews those offers to them, wherein He tells them that none of all their refusals should prejudice their acceptance with Him, in case they are willing to be His. "Turn ye at My reproof; behold, I will pour out My Spirit." And soul, the most refuse long, and stand out long against the offers of Christ and His grace ere they close with Him who are yet received and embraced by Him! Be not, therefore, discouraged, poor soul, because of your former neglects and refusals of Christ, but throw yourself into the arms of His love, which you will certainly find wide open to receive and embrace you.

5.) Is it any revolting or backsliding of yours from Him? Possibly you have sometimes been on your way towards Christ. You have had some workings, some good resolutions and affections within you for Him; aye, and you have made some profession of Him. You have, sometimes, been even upon the turning point, the point of closing with Christ, and the match has been near made up between Him and you. And yet, af-

ter all this, you have revolted and backslidden from
Him, "playing the harlot with many lovers," which
makes you fear that He will now reject you should you
go to Him. And the truth is, this also is very sad. For
hereby Christ has been eminently dishonored and your
soul has been eminently endangered. But be not discouraged, for this shall not stand between Christ and
you, if yet you are willing to be espoused to Him.

Christ offers Himself and His grace to such as
these; He promises to heal backslidings. "Thou hast
played the harlot with many lovers, yet return unto Me,
saith the Lord." And again, "Return thou backsliding
Israel, and I will not cause Mine anger to fall upon you,
for I am merciful." So Hosea 2:19, "I will betroth thee
unto Me forever; yea, I will betroth thee unto Me."
Thee? Who? Why, as revolting and backsliding a people as ever were in the world. So you will find in the
beginning of the chapter. There is hope then, you see,
for revolters and backsliders. Therefore, be not discouraged, but go to Him and He will not cast you out.

Well, soul, here is encouragement enough for you,
notwithstanding all your vileness, sinfulness, and unworthiness; and, to add to your encouragement, yet
know Christ has received multitudes that were every
way as vile, sinful, and unworthy as you are. What do
you think of Manasseh, who was a sorcerer and an
idolater? What do you think of Paul, who was a persecutor and a blasphemer? What do you think of Mary
Magdalen, who had seven devils in her? What do you
think of Rahab, who was a harlot? What do you think
of multitudes of those who crucified Christ, but afterwards believed? These were all great sinners, and yet
Christ received them into the arms of His love. What

do you think of the black list and catalogue of sinners among the Corinthians who were "drunkards, thieves, murderers, adulterers, idolaters, abusers of themselves with mankind," and the like? What do you think of them, Titus 3:3, who were "foolish, disobedient, living in envy, hateful, and hating one another, serving divers lusts and pleasures?" Surely these are as vile, as sinful, as worthless as you are, and had as much to stand between Christ and them, and yet they found grace in His sight upon looking to Him. Indeed, there is never a soul now in heaven but was, by nature, every way as vile, sinful, and unworthy of Christ as you. They lay under the same pollution. They wallowed in the same blood. They were filled with the same spirit of opposition against God and his ways that you do and are. Yea, and multitudes of them were as vile and sinful by practice also as you. They acted out the sin and enmity of their natures as highly against God and Christ as you have done; and yet these Christ received, else they would not be in heaven.

In a word, heaven, as one observes, is a house full of the miracles of Christ's free grace. There is idolatrous Manasseh among the true worshippers of God; there is the oppressing Zaccheus among the spirits of just men made perfect. There is blasphemous Paul among the host of angels, lauding, praising, and singing hallelujahs to God and the Lamb. And there is Mary Magdalen, who had seven devils, among the saints of the most high, who are filled even to overflowing with the seven spirits of God. O! who then would be discouraged? Yea, soul, all your vileness, sinfulness, and unworthiness does but, as it were, qualify you for Christ and His free grace. "My sinful wants and unworthiness," says Rutherford, "have qualified me for Christ and His grace." Cast yourself, therefore, fully upon Him, notwithstanding all, not doubting your acceptance with Him.

6. *Such is the heart of Christ, and so set upon espousal with sinners, that He delights and rejoices in nothing more than in the nuptials between Himself and them; and O, how should this draw and allure us to Him!* Should you see a young man rejoicing in the sense of an espousal between himself and such or such a one whom He loved, you might well conclude that his heart was much upon her. And is it not thus here? Christ rejoices in the sight and sense of an espousal between Himself and sinners; and how much does this argue His heart to be in the business? This I will give you in three propositions:

1.) This is what He rejoiced and delighted Himself in the thoughts of from all eternity. Thus much He Himself tells us, Proverbs 8:30-31, "Then," namely, from everlasting, "was I by Him, as one brought up with Him: and I was daily His delight; rejoicing always before Him; rejoicing in the habitable parts of the earth, and My delights were in the sons of men." These are Christ's words, and in them He tells us where He was and what He had been doing from eternity. He was with the Father and rejoiced before Him. But what did He rejoice in? Truly, next to the Father and Himself, His rejoicing was in the habitable parts of the earth, and His delights were in the sons of men. He delighted Himself in the thoughts of saving poor sinners and espousing them unto Himself in order thereunto. O how much does this argue His heart to be in the business!

2.) As He thus delighted and rejoiced in the

thoughts of it beforehand, so when at any time a poor soul is actually espoused to Him, then He rejoices afresh and is delighted afresh. Hence, the day of espousals is called "the day of gladness of His heart." The day of espousals between Christ and a poor sinner is a day of gladness and rejoicing to the Father, a day of gladness and rejoicing to the blessed Spirit, a day of gladness and rejoicing to the holy angels and spirits of just men made perfect, for there is joy in heaven at this. But it is especially a day of gladness and rejoicing to Christ the bridegroom.

O to see poor sinners come in and give up themselves to Him in a marriage covenant; this is the joy, the rest, the satisfaction of His soul! Hence it is said, "He shall see of the travail of His soul and be satisfied." It is a great grief and trouble to Christ, that which wounds His very soul, when, having wooed poor sinners, and time after time made love to them, they notwithstanding are shy of Him, and will not close with Him in a marriage covenant. Hence He complains as He does, "You will not come to Me that ye might have life; and, O Jerusalem, Jerusalem, how often would I have gathered thee, and thou wouldst not!" He speaks complainingly, and as one grieved at heart at their neglect of Him; yea, this was that which made Him weep as He did over Jerusalem. Behold the joy of the whole earth weeping! And why? Because of their refusals of Him and His grace, and the woeful destruction that for these refusals was coming upon them.

Indeed, this is what reflects great dishonor upon His name, pours great contempt upon His grace, and is indirectly contrary to the whole design of His undertaking as Mediator, and so cannot but be grievous to

Him. So, on the contrary, when souls come freely in and give up themselves in a marriage relation to Him, this gladdens and rejoices His heart. O how should this draw souls to Him! Sinner, why may not this day be made the day of the gladness of Christ's heart by being a day of espousals between Him and you? He has seen many a day of grief of heart and trouble of heart because of your standing out against Him and refusing the offers of His love. O now let Him see one day of joy of heart, and gladness of heart, by your closing with Him in a marriage covenant.

3.) As Christ delights and rejoices when souls are espoused to Him, so being espoused to Him, He delights and rejoices in this espousal forever. Men marry such or such, and they rejoice therein at present, but their joy does not last. It is otherwise with Christ; He rejoiced in the thoughts of it from all eternity; He rejoices in the being and accomplishment of it here in time, and He will rejoice in the consummation of it in heaven forever. The truth is, His joy is not complete till the marriage is complete; nor will His joy ever end till that end, which will never be (as in its place may be shown). Thus you see a little what Christ's heart is and how much set upon this business, as well as what manner of Husband He is, and what great things He does for all His spouses. And now, after all, what do you say? Are you for Christ or not? Shall the nuptial go on between Him and your souls, or shall it not? Soul, what answer must I give my Lord and Master who sent me for you?

It is but a little while, and He will call both you and me to an account concerning these things; and I must say, "Lord, I wooed that soul for Thee. I sought him to be espoused unto Thee and, as far as I was able, I displayed Thy beauty, Thy riches, Thy glory, before him. I opened Thy heart to him, showed him Thy love, and Thy willingness to be espoused to him, hoping that the cords of Thy love would draw him; and with my whole strength entreated him to give up himself in a marriage covenant to Thee."

"Well, what was the issue?"

Lord, Thou knowest. But, soul, what answer must I return? Must I be put to say, "Lord, I labored in vain and spent my strength in vain for he made light of all, and would have none either of Thee or Thy love!"

O put me not to make this dismal answer! Rather let me have cause to say, "Behold, I and the children Thou hast given me: behold, this soul, and that soul, and many souls, were won over to Thee." Amen.

Chapter 10

Which directs souls, and shows them the way how to attain unto this sweet and blessed espousal with Jesus Christ

An espousal with Christ! What could be more sweet? What could be more desirable? And who that understands Himself would not covet it before anything this world affords? No Husband like Christ, and no happiness like to an espousal to Him. But the question is, how we may attain hereunto? Truly, soul, the work is great, and it is the divine Spirit alone that does and can tie the marriage knot between Christ and you; but He works in this, as well as in other cases, in and by the use of means. And there are several things highly incumbent upon you, and which must be attended by you, if ever you would attain an acquaintance with this blessed espousal.

1. *Would you be espoused to Christ? Then labor to be deeply sensible of your utter estrangement from Him by nature; as also of your woeful state by reason of that estrangement.* A deep sense of our estrangement from Christ, and of our misery by reason of that estrangement, is one good step towards a conjugal union and relation to Him; and without the one, we are never likely to attain unto the other. Labor, therefore, for this.

Labor to be deeply sensible of your estrangement from Christ by nature. Naturally, we are all strangers to Christ; strangers to all conjugal union and communion with Him. We know not what any such thing means. As it was with the Ephesians, so it is with us all by nature; they were, and we are, without Christ in the world. And not only without Him, but also far from Him. I may truly say to every natural man and woman in this, as Peter did to Simon in another case, "Thou hast neither part nor lot in the matter." You know not what union and communion with this sweet Lord means; yea, not only are we by nature estranged from Christ, but moreover we are at enmity with Him, filled with hatred and opposition against Him. We, as those mentioned in Luke 19:14, hate Him, and would not have Him to reign over us. Naturally we are at enmity with Christ and with everything that is His—with His person, with His presence, with His Spirit, with His kingdom, with His laws and ordinances, with His righteousness, and the like. His person is too holy for us, His presence too pure, His Spirit too convincing, His kingdom too spiritual, His laws and ordinances too strict, His graces too bright, His righteousness too opposite to self; and so we hate all, and are at enmity with all; yea, we are at enmity with the very way of life and salvation by Him. "Touching the gospel, they are enemies," says the Apostle, which is spoken of the Jews, but true of all by nature. We would live, but not by Christ; we would be saved, but not by Christ. Thus, naturally we are all estranged from Him, and thus high does our estrangement rise, which we must be deeply sensible of, if ever we get union and communion in a conjugal way with Him. Therefore, work this a little upon your thoughts till you find your heart begin to bleed and relent over it.

Labor to be deeply sensible of your exceeding great

misery by reason of this estrangement. As we are all naturally without Christ, so our misery herein is exceeding great. So much the Apostle holds forth in the place before quoted, Ephesians 2:12, where he speaks of our being without Christ as our misery, yea, as the spring and foundation of all our misery; and, therefore, that is first mentioned. The Ephesians were, and we are, without the covenant, without hope, and without God in the world. Misery enough for any soul to lie under; and the inlet and foundation of all is their, and our, being without Christ. As to have Christ is the foundation of all good, so to be without Christ is the beginning and foundation of all evil, an inlet to all woe and misery, and what leaves us in a most deplorable state forever. Take a taste, and but a taste, of this your misery, and then work the sense of it upon your own souls.

1.) Being without Christ, you are destitute of all good. You are without life, without grace, without peace, without pardon, without comfort, without righteousness, without heaven, without salvation, without hope, and without God, without the favor, without the presence, without the life, without the image, without the Spirit of God. And being thus without God, you are without all true good and true happiness. According to the old and true maxim, "without the chief good, there is nothing good."

2.) Being without Christ, you are in bondage to sin and Satan, which is the worst bondage in the world. Naturally, we are all the slaves and vassals of these cruel lords. Hence we are said to fulfill the devil's lusts; and, as the lusts of the devil, so the will and lusts of the flesh to be the servants of sin, and to serve divers lusts and

pleasures, and the like. And, as naturally all are thus in
bondage to sin and the devil, so there is no redemption from this bondage but by Christ, and that in a way
of union with Him. "If the Son shall make you free, ye
shall be free indeed," saith He Himself to the Jews.
They were glorying in their privilege that they were
Abraham's seed and never were in bondage to any
man. True, says Christ, but you are in a worse bondage
than a bondage to man—in bondage to sin, in
bondage to your lusts—for "he that committeth sin is
the servant of sin." And this bondage none but the Son
can free you from; and, therefore, until freed by Him,
you remain under it. O how sore a bondage is this, to
be under the command of sin, to be at the beck of every base and unclean lust, and to be carried captive by
the devil at His will! This is such a bondage that the
bondage of Israel under their taskmasters in Egypt,
and the bondage of Turkish slaves who are kept at the
oar and galley, is freedom compared to it. As to serve
Christ is the greatest liberty, so to serve sin is the cru-
elest bondage.

3.) Being without Christ, and union with Christ,
you are rejected by God. "Know ye not," says the Apostle, "that except Christ be in you, ye are reprobates?"

"Know ye not?" as if He should say, "It is a most
clear, manifest, and evident truth that, unless you have
union with Christ, you are reprobates"; that is, you are
unapproved of God; you are out of His favor; both
your persons and services are rejected by Him. O how
sad does this speak your condition to be! For men, yea,
for good men to reject and disown us is what may be
borne, especially when God owns and smiles; but for
God to disown and reject us, this is terrible indeed,

though all the world should own us, and smile upon us. How terrible is that word? "Reprobate silver shall call for them, for the Lord hath rejected them." If God owns and smiles, it does not matter who frowns; but if He frowns and rejects, who can own or smile to the relief of the soul?

4.) Being without Christ, you are under the law, and so under the curse. And how sad is this! As there are but two covenants, the Old and the New, and but two heads of those covenants, the first and second Adam, so all men do belong to, and are found in, the one or other of these. While, therefore, you are strangers to Christ, you are under the law; and, being under the law, you are under the curse, for, says the Apostle, "As many as are under the law, are under the curse; for it is written, cursed is every one that continueth not in all things that are written in the book of the law, to do them." The law has no pity, no sparing for offenders, but for every breach thereof lays the soul under the curse.

Now we have all broken the law; we all broke it in Adam, being in him as in a head; and we have all broken it ten thousand times over in our own persons, and by both are fallen under the curse thereof. And soul, do you know what the curse of the law means? It carries in it death and condemnation forever. Being under the law, we are cursed in our persons and cursed in our comforts; the wrath of God lies upon our souls, and the curse of God is in all our enjoyments; our very blessings are accursed to us, Malachi 2:2.

5.) Being without Christ and estranged from Christ, you lie under the guilt of innumerable sins, which you alone must bear forever. It is in and by

Christ alone that souls are discharged from the guilt of sin. And who are they whom He discharges from guilt but such as are found in Him, who are under a marriage covenant with Him? Those His blood cleansed from all sin, and in Him have they redemption through His blood, even the forgiveness of sin. As for others, He tells them plainly that they shall die in their sins. O how sad a condition is this! Soul, you are guilty of a multitude of sins, the least of which has evil enough in it to damn you eternally. You have thousands, and ten thousands, of scarlet, crimson sins, sins clothed with black and crying aggravations lying upon you; and to have all these in the full weight of the guilt and punishment of them, charged upon you by the great God forever, how miserable does this speak your condition to be!

6.) Being estranged from Christ, you have nothing to satisfy divine justice, which is ready to seize upon you; nothing to pacify divine wrath, which is ready to break forth against you; nothing to stand between divine revenge and your sinful souls. What shall I say? You have many accusers and, by them, many heavy charges brought against you; and being without Christ, you have no advocate to plead your cause, none to speak a good word in heaven for you. And is that not sad? You are deeply in debt. You owe your ten thousand talents to divine justice. And being without Christ, you have nothing to pay but are in danger of being cast into the prison of eternal darkness from whence there is no redemption. And is that not sad? You are under an obligation to much duty; and, being without Christ, you are under an utter impossibility of performing any of it acceptably. You are under a judgment of condemnation, and, being without Christ, you have nothing that can secure you one day, one hour, one moment more this side of everlasting burnings; and O how sad and miserable is this! Thus you see both your estrangement from Christ and also your misery, in part, by reason of that estrangement. Now, as ever you would get union and communion with Him, labor to be deeply sensible of both these.

2. *Would you indeed be espoused to Christ? Then labor to be soundly convinced and deeply sensible of the greatness and heinousness of the sin of refusing Christ and the offers of His love.* Poor soul, you stand out against Christ; He woos, calls, and invites you to Himself, but you slight and refuse all; but let me tell you, this is a most heinous and crying sin. To swear, to murder, to steal, to be drunk, to be unclean and the like, these you look upon as black and horrid things. Indeed, well you may, for they are sins of more than an ordinary heinous and abominable nature. But you know that your sin in rejecting Christ and the offers of His love is greater and more provoking than all these. This, indeed, is the great sin, and the sin you must, in a special manner, be sensible of if ever you are united to Christ. So much Christ Himself tells us in that place, John 16:8-9: "He shall convince the world of sin, because they believe not in Me." Unbelief, then, is the great "sin" that the Spirit convinces souls of. And what is unbelief, but the neglect and refusal of Christ and the offers of His love made to us in the gospel? "He shall convince the world of sin, because they believe not in Me"; that is, He shall convince the world of that grand sin of unbelief, as a learned man expounds it. As if Christ should say, "He

shall make men see the black and heinous nature of the sin of rejecting Me and My love. He shall humble them for it, and set them a bleeding over it."

This sin of rejecting Christ some of the schoolmen have called the greatest sin of all; and, indeed, next to the unpardonable sin, what greater? This is a sin most directly and immediately against Christ and the gospel. O! for a vile, wretched sinner to shut the door of his soul against Christ, the King of glory, and deny Him entertainment; to refuse and reject the frequent offers of Him and His love, how great a sin must this be? And, soul, to convince you the better of it, I shall suggest a few considerations to you, holding forth a little of its black and horrid evil.

1.) Consider that the neglect and refusal of Christ and His love is a sin against a special and eminent command, and, therefore, a great and crying sin. The greater and more eminent the command is which we transgress and sin against, the greater our sin and guilt is in transgressing that command. Now, God not only commands us to receive and embrace Christ and His love, but this command of His is a great, signal, and eminent command. So St. John tells us, "This is His commandment, that we believe on the name of His Son Jesus Christ, whom He hath sent." What is it to believe on the name of Jesus Christ but to receive and embrace Christ offering Himself in the gospel to us and live upon Him, having so received and embraced Him? Now, says He, "This is the commandment," His great, His special commandment, in a most signal and eminent manner; and Christ Himself asserts the same thing, John 6:28-29. In the 28th verse, they ask Him, "What shall we do that we may work the works of God?"

His answer in the 29th verse is, "This is the work of God, that ye believe on Him whom He hath sent"; that is, that you receive and embrace Me, and live upon Me by believing. This is the work of God, the great work which He commands you and expects from you. Believing, as Calvin observes upon this place, is not called the work of God because it is of God's operation (as you have it elsewhere), or that which God works in us, but because it is the great thing which He commands and requires of us.

To reject and refuse Christ, then, is a sin against a signal and eminent command, indeed, against the great command of the gospel. And, therefore, it must be a great and crying sin. More particularly, the neglect and refusal of Christ and His love is a sin against a clear and express command of God, a command wherein the authority of God peculiarly and eminently shines forth. So much is held forth in the place mentioned before, John 6:29, "This is the commandment" (speaking of the commandment of faith), His express commandment, a commandment wherein His authority is evidently and peculiarly seen. The authority of God shines forth in all His commands, but especially in this above the rest; therefore, this you see has an emphasis put upon it; "This is His commandment." Now, the more clearly and eminently the authority of God shines forth in any command, the greater our sin and guilt is in transgressing that command.

The neglect and refusal of Christ and His love is a sin against a command wherein the heart of God and Christ much lies and is, therefore, a great sin. This is a rule, that the more the mind or heart of the Lawgiver is in any law or command, the greater is our sin and guilt in the breach and transgression of that law or command. Now, God's command to us to receive Christ by believing is a command wherein His own heart, as well as the heart of Christ, much lies; indeed, there is nothing in all the world that the heart of God and Christ is more set upon, or desirous of, than this: that souls should embrace Christ by believing, and become one with Him in a marriage covenant. Witness the freeness of their offers, the frequency of their calls, the importunateness of their pleas, the patientness of their waitings, the affectionateness of their entreaties, the friendliness of their upbraidings, the patheticalness of their lamentings, the sweetness of their wooings, the unweariedness of their drawings, and the graciousness of their dealings in reference hereunto. But you have already seen how much the heart of Christ, and in Him the heart of the Father, is in this business. Now, to transgress such a command, a command wherein the heart of God and Christ so much lies, and to run counter to that which they much desire, O what a sin must this needs be!

The neglect and refusal of Christ is a sin against a command which has virtually all the commands of God in it; and so, in the breach and transgression thereof, we break and transgress all. And O how great a sin must this be! To believe on Christ is comprehensive of all that God commands and requires of us. This is so much His commandment that, in obeying this, we obey all; and, in violating this, we violate all; and so He esteems and accounts it. This is evident from John 6:28-29, "What shall we do, say they, that we may work the works of God? This is the work of God," says Christ, "to believe on Him whom He hath sent." Pray mark, they speak of works in the plural number. They would know what all these works were which God required and what the extent of the command was. And Christ, in His answer, reduces all to one, and that is faith; by which He shows that as all is in vain without faith, so faith is virtually all that God requires. "This is the work of God," says He. As if He should say, "Here is all in one, to believe on and receive Me is comprehensive of all." And accordingly, my beloved, to reject Christ and His love is to break all at once, to violate all at once. It is to rebel against, and pour contempt upon, the whole mind and will of God at once, and, in effect, to renounce all duty and allegiance to Him. Suitable whereunto is the observation of a learned man upon that place, John 16:8-9. Christ here calls unbelief sin simply and absolutely, because that sin comprehends all sin in it. O how great a sin then must this be!

The neglect and refusal of Christ is a sin against a command of much love. All God's commands have love in them; they are designed by Him for our good, as the Scripture tells us, but especially this command of His, that we should receive and embrace His Son; for what is this command but a command to us to be saved, a command to us to be happy? What is this but a commanding of us to live forevermore, to be eternally blessed and with Himself? And how great a sin must the transgression of such a command be! Did God command us any hard or severe thing, something that tended to our prejudice and not our happiness, that would be something; but when He commands us nothing but to be happy, and to be happy in the best way, O how great a sin must it be to transgress such a command!

2.) Consider the neglect and refusal of Christ is a sin which, in a peculiar manner, derogates and pours great contempt upon Him, and, therefore, is a great sin. The more contempt any sin pours upon Christ, and the more it derogates Him, the greater that sin is. Now, what sin derogates more from Christ, or pours greater contempt upon Him, than the neglect and refusal of Him offering Himself to us does? This is a sin which takes the crown from off Christ's head and throws it in the dust; every way, and in all respects, it pours great contempt upon Him.

This sin vilifies and pours contempt upon the person of Christ. Christ's person is infinitely amiable and, accordingly, to vilify and condemn His person must be a great sin and contract great guilt; and this refusal of Him does, hence it is called a treading under foot the Son of God, which argues the highest contempt imaginable. Every refusal of Christ carries that language concerning Him in it: "When we see Him there is no beauty in Him, for which we should desire Him; He has neither form nor comeliness in Him." He is a person of no worth, of no desirableness. O what contempt is this to be cast upon Christ! And how does this derogate Him!

This sin vilifies and pours contempt upon the work, office, and undertaking of Christ as Mediator, upon all that He has done and suffered, with all the riches of His grace and His love manifested therein. Hence it is called as a treading of the Son of God under foot; so an accounting His blood as a common and unholy thing; a thing of no worth, no use, no value, no excellency. Great, my beloved, was the work and undertaking of Christ as our Mediator, and great were the things which He both did and suffered in the discharge of that work and undertaking. Great also was His grace and love towards us in all; and, accordingly, great must our sin and guilt be in pouring contempt thereon, which we do by our refusing Him. Hereby we pour contempt upon all His acts and all His offices as Mediator, upon all His merits and all His purchases, upon all His grace and love in bleeding and dying for us. We do hereby in effect say that neither Christ, nor anything which He has purchased, is worth accepting and embracing, that we would rather that He had never died, never become a day's-man between God and us, that He might have kept His blood to Himself, and we will not thank Him for shedding it, that we need neither Him nor anything that is His. Hereby we, in effect, say that the whole gospel is a cheat, a lie, a mere delusion, that Christ is a hard Master and rules with rigor, that salvation is little worth, and the like. O what horrid contempt of Christ is this!

This sin plainly prefers a poor, base, vile lust before Christ and all the glorious riches and treasures of Christ. And O what contempt of Christ is this! Why do men refuse Christ and the offers of His love? Surely it is for the sake and from the love of some lust or other; either the lust of the flesh, the lust of the eye, or the pride of life; and if so, then by refusing Him, they really prefer this lust before Him and all the treasures of His grace and love. And thus indeed you find it to be, Matthew 22; as also Luke 14:18-20, where Christ offers Himself with all His treasures to poor sinners who yet slight and refuse both Him and them. And why so? The one has a farm, the other a merchandise, and all have some carnal concern to mind. The sum is, they

have a lust to be satisfied; and, therefore, Christ and all
the treasures of His love must be rejected. By refusing
Christ, in effect we say that there is more good, more
sweetness, more happiness in a lust, in a little carnal,
worldly pleasure and advantage, than there is in Christ
and all that is His. Hereby, in effect, we say that men
are deceived in Christ, that the Word of God makes a
false report of Him, that He is not such a Savior, nor is
His salvation so great as the one and the other is represented to be. O what contempt is this to be cast upon
Christ! Esau is said to despise his birthright. And how?
By preferring a mess of porridge or a morsel of meat
before it. But O how much more do we condemn
Christ and His love by preferring a base, vile lust before Him! Surely, greater contempt than this cannot
well be found. And how great, then, must the sin of the
refusal of Christ be! And how much should we tremble
at it!

3.) Consider that the neglect and refusal of
Christ is a sin which, in an eminent manner, darkens
and opposes the glory of God, and reflects the highest
dishonor upon Him of all other, and is, therefore, a
great sin. The more any sin darkens and opposes the
glory of God, the greater the guilt of that sin is; for,
first, the more any sin opposes the glory of God, and
reflects dishonor upon Him, the more contrary it is to
the highest good; the greater the guilt of it must needs
be. And, secondly, the more any sin opposes the glory
of God and reflects dishonor upon Him, the more it
thwarts and contradicts the highest end of man; and
the more any sin thwarts and contradicts the highest
end of man, the greater the guilt of that sin is.

Now, the neglect and refusal of Christ is what eminently opposes the glory of God and reflects dishonor upon Him; the reception and entertainment of Christ puts an honor upon the Father. Indeed, every act of faith honors God; and, especially, this great and fundamental act of faith in embracing Christ. So, on the other hand, the neglect and refusal of Christ is what reflects dishonor upon God and throws His glory in the dust. And hence it is that this sin is so exceedingly provoking to Him, as in the Scripture it is represented to be. Particularly, take here two things:

First, this sin of refusing Christ is what slights and condemns the glorious excellencies and perfections of God at once, and so cannot but cast very great dishonor upon Him and be very opposite to His glory in Christ. My beloved, all the glorious excellencies and perfections of God are eminently manifested and displayed. In Him all the glorious counsels of His grace and love meet; and, in refusing Him, we despise and pour contempt upon all. In Him His love eminently shines forth and the fullness of it rests. In Him are justice, righteousness, and holiness eminently manifested and displayed. In Him His wisdom, yea, His manifold wisdom, appears and reveals itself. In a word, the whole God is manifest and revealed in Him, and withal offered to the embraces of our faith and love; in every offer of Christ made to us in the gospel, God does, in effect, say to us, "Whatever I am or can do as God, that I will be for you to make you happy forever."

Accordingly, to refuse Christ must pour contempt upon all; it slights and pours contempt upon the grace of God, the wisdom of God, the power of God, the justice of God, the holiness of God, the fullness and all-sufficiency of God, and all the ancient, glorious coun-

sels of His love concerning souls. To refuse Christ is in
effect to say that the grace of God is no grace, at least
not worthy of our acceptance; that His justice and holiness are not to be regarded and that we value them
not; that His wisdom is folly and His power weakness;
that His fullness has little in it, and is no way able to
satisfy us and make us happy; that a broken cistern is as
good as that fountain of living waters and, hereby, we
downright deny His faithfulness and put the lie upon
Him. In effect we say that the God of truth is a liar, that
His witness and testimony is not to be credited, that
His word of promise is a mere delusion and for no
other use than to beguile souls. O what contempt, what
dishonor must all this cast upon the blessed God, and
what horrible wickedness must it be! "To make God a
liar," says a learned man, "is horrible and execrable
impiety; thereby we take that from Him which is most
dear and proper to Him." O tremble, soul, tremble at
the blackness and hellishness of this sin!

Second, this sin of refusing Christ is what is directly
opposite to the highest design of God for His own
glory, and robs Him of that glory which is most dear to
Him. What, my beloved, was the highest design that
ever God laid and carried on for His own glory? Verily,
it was Christ, and the salvation of sinners by Christ. He
designed Himself a revenue of glory in making the
world, and He designs Himself a revenue of glory in all
He does in governing the world. But that wherein He
has designed the highest revenue of glory to Himself is
the mystery of Christ and salvation by Christ. So much
is evident from Ephesians 1:11-14, "In whom," says he,
speaking of Christ, "we have obtained an inheritance,
being predestinated according to the purpose of Him,

who worketh all things after the counsel of His own
will, that we should be to the praise of His glory." And
again, verse 14, "unto the praise of His glory." The sum
is this, that God's glory was His great end in the dispensation of Christ and our salvation by Him; and also
that in and by that He designed the highest revenue of
glory to Himself. For pray observe, first, He calls it "the
praise of His glory," the splendor and highest emana-
tion of His glory. Second, He repeats this design of
God to "the praise of His glory"; and again, "to the
praise of His glory," which notes this to be His grand
design for His glory. And again, what is that glory that
is most near to God? Verily it is the glory of His grace.

Grace is His darling attribute, and the glory of His
grace is most dear to Him. Hence this has been peculiarly His design in the whole of the mystery of Christ.
So the same Apostle tells us, Ephesians 1:6, who, having before spoken of the great mysteries of predestina-
tion and redemption by Christ, here in verse 6 tells you
what was God's great design in all, namely, "the praise
of the glory of His grace." It is the crowning of grace
and the enthroning of grace which God, in a peculiar
manner, delights in. Now, if the highest design of God
for His own glory is by the mystery of Christ and our
salvation by Christ, and the glory of His grace is most
dear to Him, then it is clear that our refusal of Christ is
most opposite to the highest design that God ever carried on for His own glory and robs Him of that glory
which is most dear to Him; for alas! this is in effect to
say that God has laid out no grace upon sinners in the
dispensation of Christ, and that He deserves no glory
upon the account of that dispensation. This is, in effect, to tell Him that neither Christ nor His grace in

Him is worth minding, worth receiving, and that we are in no ways beholden to Him for the one or the other. And O what dishonor must this reflect upon God, and how darkening to His glory! And, accordingly, soul, let you and me tremble at it, and at the blackness and horridness of that sin that has such a dreadful effect.

4.) Consider that the neglect and refusal of Christ is a sin which directly and immediately murders the soul and damns it eternally, and, therefore, must be a great sin. That sin that most directly and immediately murders the soul and destroys it eternally must be a great sin and should be greatly dreaded by us. And what sin is it that does this but our neglect and refusal of Christ? And, soul, that you may be the more deeply convinced of this, seriously weigh these following propositions:

The neglect and refusal of Christ is a sin which rejects the only remedy of sinful souls. Poor sinners are, in themselves, dead, lost, undone, and perishing forever. They are sick, and sick to death. They are sinful, and sinful to damnation. And there is one, and only one, remedy for them and that is Christ—Christ and His blood, Christ and His grace, Christ and His fullness. Besides this, "There is no balm in Gilead, no physician there for them; neither is there salvation in any other." Therefore, by refusing and rejecting Him, they refuse and reject the only remedy. He indeed is a complete, as well as an only, remedy. He is able, and as willing as He is able, to save to the very uttermost, as the Scripture tells us. But they, by rejecting Him, exclude themselves from His saving efficacy and so, thereby, directly murder their own souls.

The neglect and refusal of Christ is a sin which binds all a man's other sins fast to Him. It is a great and weighty saying which a worthy divine has, "Unbelief (which is properly the neglect and refusal of Christ) binds all a man's sins fast to His soul, and damnation fast to his sins." It is, indeed, the bond of all our guilt and all our misery, that which makes the curse cleave close to us forever; and, while a man remains in this sin, it is impossible that he should be acquitted and discharged from the guilt of any one of all his sins. It is Augustine's observation upon that place, John 16:8-9, where Christ tells us that His Spirit shall convince the world of sin, because they believe not in Him. "Christ," says he, "instances in the sin of infidelity in a special manner, because that sin remaining, all our other sins remain; but that being taken away, all others are forgiven." Faith blots out all sins, but unbelief binds all fast upon us. Hence that word of Christ, "If ye believe not ye shall die in your sins"; that is, your sins shall cleave close to you to the very death. This will be further evident in the next proposition.

That though all sin is killing and damning, yet no sin shall ever damn or destroy us unless we add thereunto the sin of neglect or refusal of Christ. It is true, every sin is damning; sin within, sin without. "The wages of sin is death"; and the Apostle tells us, "There is a just recompence of reward due to every transgression and disobedience." But though every sin is damning, yet whatever a man's sins are, though never so many, never so great, they shall never, they can never damn Him if He receives and embraces Christ. Nor, indeed, can any of all a man's sins be said to be the immediate cause of His damnation except His refusing

Christ. Indeed, under the law the immediate cause of man's perishing was sin in general; but under the gospel the only immediate cause of men's perishing is the rejection of Christ and His grace through unbelief. So much Christ Himself tells us in John 3:18: "He that believeth on the Son is not condemned; but He that believeth not is condemned already, because He hath not believed on the name of the only begotten Son of God." He that believes on Christ is not condemned. And why so? Is it because he has no sins to condemn him? No, but because, believing on Christ, all his sins are done away; but he that does not believe on Him is condemned already! And why? Is it because he is a sinner in general, or because his sins are many and great sins? No, but "because he hath not believed on the name of the only begotten Son of God." The sum of all this is that the immediate cause of man's condemnation is not this sin or that sin, but their refusing Christ by unbelief. Hence you have it so frequently up and down the gospel, "He that believeth shall be saved; he that believeth not shall be damned," and the like. Well, then, if our refusing of Christ is the rejecting of the only remedy of sinful souls, if it is what binds all a man's sins fast upon him, and if none of all a man's other sins, though many and great, should or could ever damn him, were not this sin of refusing Christ added to them; then, certainly, this is that which most directly and immediately murders the soul. O how great a sin, then, does this speak it to be! Murder is a great sin, an iniquity to be punished by the judge; nor do we look upon a murderer fit to live. But no murder is like a soul murder, nor should we suffer this soul murderer to live one moment.

5.) Consider that the neglect and refusal of Christ is a sin which argues you to be really in love with your sins, which truly and indeed chooses death rather than life, loves darkness more than light, and which leaves you without the least color of excuse or room of appeal forever. And O what a black and horrid sin must this then be! A little of each:

(1) This sin of neglecting and refusing Christ is what really argues you to be in love with your sins and to have slight thoughts of them. For men to act on sin is bad, but to have slight thoughts of sin and to be in love with it is much worse. Sin, being against an infinite good, ever infinitely contrary to the blessed God, has infinite evil in it. O how dreadful a thing is this! Yet this your refusal of Christ carries in it; for pray mark, if you did not have slight thoughts of sin, you would not refuse the pardon of sin when offered you but would account it worthy of all acceptance; and were you not in love with your sins, yea, greatly in love with them, you would not choose and desire to continue in your sins; much less would you refuse and reject so great a good as Christ is for the sake of your sins. Should a condemned malefactor refuse the king's free pardon, would not this argue him to have slight thoughts of death, yea, to be in love with it and to prefer it before life? As clearly does your refusing of Christ argue you to have slight thoughts of sin and to be in love with it. O were you not in love with your sins, you would be glad of a discharge and deliverance from them, and would, with all readiness and joyfulness, embrace it when freely offered to you as in Christ it is!

(2) This sin of refusing Christ is what truly and indeed speaks you to love darkness more than

light and to choose death rather than life. It is what prefers sin and death before Christ, life, and grace. O what a black sin then must it be! This Christ Himself asserts concerning it, and that as a high aggravation of it and what makes it doubly damning, "This is the condemnation, that light is come into the world, and men love darkness rather than light." Christ and the good things of Christ are here called "light." On the other hand, sin and death, sin and the miseries that attend it, are called "darkness."

"Now," says Christ, "men, by unbelief and refusing Me, declare that they love this darkness before this light; men, by refusing Me, in effect love, choose, prefer sin, death, and darkness before Me and My grace, Me and that eternal life which I would give them." O what a sin is this! Christ may truly say to sinners, as Moses said to them of old, Deuteronomy 30:19, "I call heaven and earth to record this day against you, that I have set before you life and death, blessing and cursing: therefore choose life that ye may live." Now, for them to choose death and reject life, to choose the curse, and reject the blessing, is a dreadful sin indeed; and the mode is dreadful, on the one hand, because the light is so lovely and amiable. And, on the other hand, the darkness is so hideous and terrible, as also the obligations which lie upon us to love, choose, and prefer the light before darkness are so weighty and forcible. Christ earnestly desires it and He graciously counsels it. He strictly commands it and no less than a whole eternity of glorious and unspeakable happiness depends upon it. O think of these things!

(3) The sin of refusing Christ is a sin which leaves you without the least color or excuse or room of

appeal forever, which must argue it to be a great sin indeed.

First, it leaves you without the least color of excuse for sin, and without the least color of excuse why you should not die for sin. This Christ Himself expresses in John 15:22, "If I had not come and spoken unto them, they had not had sin; but now they have no cloak for their sin." That is, "If I had not come and spoken to them (namely, in the gospel), revealing My Father's will and offering Myself and My grace to them, they had not had sin; that is, not so great sin. But now they have no cloak, no excuse for their sin. Now they have no pretense to make, nothing wherewith to color or extenuate their sin." The neglect and refusal of Christ leaves men altogether inexcusable, and it will do so, to be sure, in the last day. O when God, in the day of His righteous judgment, shall demand of men who have lived under the gospel why they sin, and have sinned; why they are found in their sins; and, being found in their sins, why they should not die forever, what will they have to say by way of excuse or apology for themselves? Verily, nothing, but they will be speechless.

They cannot say they were not warned of the evil of sin. They cannot say that pardon and salvation were not offered to them. They cannot say that the offer was not full, free, and clear. They cannot say they had to do with a hard Master, nor can they say that sin is not worthy of death. They will have nothing to say.

Second, it leaves you without the least of room of appeal forever. I may say here, as it is said in another case, 1 Samuel 2:25, "If one man sin against another, the judge shall judge him; but if a man sin against the Lord, who shall entreat for him?" So, if a man sins

against the law by trangressing it, he may appeal to the
gospel and the grace of Christ there; but, if a man sins
against Christ and His grace offered in the gospel,
where then shall he appeal? Verily, there is no appeal
to be made, no relief to be found for him. If a man is
condemned at the seat of justice as having sinned
against the law, He may appeal unto the mercy-seat,
the throne of grace, and find sweet relief; but, if he
sins against the mercy seat and the throne of grace,
then he has nothing to appeal to that may administer
relief to him. Now, by refusing Christ, we sin against
the throne of grace. We pull down, as much as in us
lies, the mercy seat; and where then shall we appeal? O
consider these things, and learn by them to dread this
sin of refusing Christ! I might say much more to convince you of the heinous evil of it, but let this suffice.
Sure I am it is enough too. And, had we the due sense
of it upon our spirits, it would make us tremble at it
forever.

3. *Would you indeed be espoused to Christ? Then do not
give way to the discouragement of sense, but bear up your soul
upon the encouragements of faith, upon such gospel principles
and considerations as tend to draw sinners to faith in Christ.*
Possibly, upon reading and considering the woeful
misery of your condition without Christ and the dreadful heinousness of your sin and guilt in your long and
frequent refusing of Him, discouragements (not a few)
may arise within. And, indeed, no sooner usually does
a poor soul look towards Christ or think of closing with
Him in a marriage covenant but immediately multitudes of discouragements arise to deter Him there-
from. "O," says he, "what a monstrous sinner I am!

How have I despised Christ and His grace! How long
have I stood it out against Him! I have served my lusts
all my days, and rejected His calls. To what purpose do
I now talk of closing with Him?" These, and multitudes
of such like discouragements, arise in the soul which,
being given way to, effectually keep him from Christ.
But if ever, soul, you would attain to union and communion with Him, you must shut your eyes and heart
too against all discouragements of this nature; and,
though they press upon you again and again, yet thrust
them out, fixing your eye and heart upon the encouragements of faith. Dwell much in the thoughts of
them, and bear up your soul upon such gospel principles and considerations as tend to weaken unbelief and
beget faith in the soul. And, for your help herein, I
shall mention some of these encouragements of faith,
or gospel principles, which I would have you to be se-
rious and frequent in the contemplation of.

     1.) The first gospel principle or encouragement
of faith which you should bear your soul upon, and be
frequent in the contemplation of, is this: there is a
rich, a glorious, and an overflowing fullness of all good
treasured up in Christ for poor sinners, and His grace
abundantly exceeds both our wants and sins. It is the
work and nature of unbelief to belittle and limit the
fullness of Christ in the eye of the soul. It shows the
soul the multitude of his sins and wants, but conceals
and locks up Christ's treasure and fullness. And whatever we pretend the ground of our not closing with
Christ is, at least one principle is that we doubt His
fullness. We do not see enough in Christ to supply all
our wants and relieve our distresses, unbelief persuading us that Christ is not the Christ the Scripture repre-

sents Him to be. But soul, away with all such apprehensions, and swell in the contemplation of Christ's infinite fullness. Look to Him as one infinitely able to supply your wants, to pardon your sins, to heal your maladies, to subdue your lusts, to sanctify your heart, and to save your soul eternally. Look upon Him as the Scripture represents Him. It pleased the Father that in Him should all fulness dwell—all fullness of grace and life, of peace and pardon, of righteousness and salvation. There is in Christ not only a fullness of abundance but of redundance, an overflowing fullness, a fullness infinitely superabounding our sins and wants. The Scripture tells us that "He is able to save unto the very uttermost all that come unto God by Him"—save, able to save, and able to save to the uttermost! And not one or two but *all* who come unto God by Him.

The Scripture speaks of Christ's "unsearchable riches." The ocean of His grace in not to be sounded by the longest line of the largest created understanding. Paul experienced the superabounding fullness of grace, and has left it upon record for our encouragement. 1 Timothy 1:14, "The grace of our Lord was exceeding abundant." It was more than enough. I found more grace in Christ (as one expresses it) than I know what to do with. And yet what was Paul? He himself tells you in the verse before and after that he was a blasphemer, a persecutor, and the chief of sinners, a man every way of as many sins and wants as you are. Accordingly, view him and bear up your soul in the face of discouragement. Reason thus with yourself: "True, my condition is sad, my wants are many, and my sins exceedingly great. But what then? Is there no balm in Gilead? Is there no physician there? Is not Christ

able to save me, and that to the uttermost, notwithstanding all? Look, O my soul, yonder is Jesus upon the
throne at the Father's right hand, full of grace and
truth. Look upon Him and consider, what are all your
wants to His riches and fullness? What are all your miseries and distresses to His bowels of mercy? What are
all your sins to the merit of His blood? Your provocations to His satisfaction? Were your wants more and
greater than they are, His fullness could supply them
all. Were your sins greater and more heinous than they
are, His blood could cleanse you from all. 'The blood
of Jesus Christ cleanseth from all sin.' There is infinitely more worth in His merits to pardon and justify
you than there is evil in your sins to damn and destroy
you. True, I have a fountain of sin, guilt, and death in
me, but here is a deeper fountain of grace and life and
righteousness in Him. See, O my soul, see how vast and
large His treasures of grace and glory are, and bear up
yourself upon them."

O if sinners dwelt more in the view of the glorious
fulness of Christ they would be more in love with Him,
and hereby would counterwork and undermine unbelief in one of its greatest artifices whereby it keeps souls
from Him. I shall here, for your encouragement only,
subjoin the saying of a worthy divine, "Christ can, and
it becomes Him well to, give more than your narrow
soul can conceive. Christ is a well of life, but who
knows how deep it is to the bottom?"

2.) The second gospel principle or encouragement of faith which you should bear up your soul
upon, and be frequent in the contemplation of, is this:
that as there is such a glorious and inexhaustable fullness in Christ, so this fullness is in Him, not for

Himself, but to be dispensed and communicated to
poor souls coming to Him. "True," may the soul say,
"here is fullness enough, riches and treasures enough,
of all good in Christ, but what is this to me? Or
wherein does it concern me?"

Wherein does it concern you? Why, it is wholly your
concern, and the concern of such as you are. For whatever fullness He has in Him, it is treasured in Him for
sinners, yea, for the worst of sinners. How sweet is that
word, Psalm 68:18, where, speaking of Christ, the Holy
Ghost tells us that He has received gifts for men. He
has received gifts, that is, He has a fullness of all good
in His hand, and at His disposal, and this for men.

"Aye, but I am a devil," says the soul, "a rebel, and
what is this to me?"

Observe what follows, and you will find it concerns
you, yea, you especially: "He hath received gifts for
men, yea, for the rebellious also." Hence also it is that
He is said to be made Head over all things to the
church, Ephesians 1:22. He has all fullness dwelling in
Him, but it is a Head, and so it is all for the use and
service of the body, for every poor soul that comes to
Him; and therefore it is added, "Head over all things
to the church," that is, for the church's use and service,
of which He is Head. Take a view of all that fullness
that is in Christ, and it is all as much and as really for
the use and service of such as come to Him and are
made members of His body as the treasures and en-
dowments of the natural head are for the use and service of the natural body and the members thereof. And
O what encouragement is this to faith! It is the observation of a learned man upon the place last quoted,
"Lest we should think this great glory of Christ to be a

thing that does not concern us, He is here declared to
be constituted by the Father to be the Head of the
whole church." Well then, soul, bear up yourself upon
this encouragement. Say, "Look, O my soul, look unto
Jesus who has received gifts for men. View Him as one
that has received a fullness of all grace from the Father
on purpose to be dispensed and communicated to you
and such as you are. He has life in Him, and He has it
for you; He has peace and pardon in Him, and He has
it for you; He has wisdom and righteousness, grace and
glory in Him, and He has it for you; and such as you
are. And therefore, go to Him, expect all from Him."

3.) The third gospel principle or encouragement of faith which you should bear up your soul
upon, and dwell much in the contemplation of, is this:
that there is a perfect freedom and willingness in
Christ. Yea, it is even genuine and natural to Him to
bestow Himself, with all His glorious riches and fullness, upon poor souls coming to Him. Christ has all
this fullness in Him as a Head; so you have it expressly
stated in Colossians 1:18-19.

Now, as it is genuine and natural to the head to
minister influence to the members, so it is even genuine and natural to Christ to communicate His grace
to poor souls. It is the way and work of the devil and
unbelief to persuade poor souls that Christ will not receive them, nor communicate His grace and fullness to
them though they should come to Him, which they
endeavor to do from the consideration of His greatness and holiness, together with their vileness and sinfulness. Christ, they say, is choice and peculiar in His
love and respects, as great persons used to be. He will
know His distance, and He will make sinners know

theirs; but, soul, deal with this as from the devil and unbelief; reject it as a reproach thrown upon Christ, and dwell much in the contemplation of His infinite willingness to receive and save the worst of sinners that come to Him. Reason it a little with yourself: Why did He become incarnate? Why did He bleed and die? Why does He woo, wait, offer, call, and strive with poor sinners to win them to Himself? Does it not all argue a willingness and readiness in Him to give forth both Himself and His fullness to them?

4.) The fourth gospel principle or encouragement of faith which you should bear up your soul upon, and dwell much in the contemplation of, is this: the only spring and principle of all that ever Christ does for poor sinners, from first to last, is from His own sovereign grace and love. It was His love that brought Him down from heaven and led Him out to bleed and die for them. Hence, in Ephesians 5:25, He is said to love His church and give Himself for her. It is His love, His free love, that first draws them to Himself and allures them into covenant with Him. "I have loved you with an everlasting love, therefore with loving-kindness have I drawn thee." It is His love that receives them, that pardons them, that bestows life and salvation upon them. Hence, all is said to be of grace, even the whole of our salvation. Hence He is represented to us as sitting upon a throne of grace, and there it is that He invites us to come to Him, and from thence gives out all to us; and, therefore, to that throne we, though sinners, may come boldly. He is upon a throne and, therefore, we may assure ourselves that He will do great things for sinners coming to Him. He will act like a king, pardon like a king, save like a king, do all with

kingly grace and magnificence. And it is a throne of
grace, a throne that reigns grace, a throne whereon
grace sits in imperial majesty, and decrees all for poor
sinners coming to it; and so does all freely, all in a way
of sovereign grace and love. Hence that language, "I
will have mercy because I will have mercy." I will pardon because I will pardon. I will save because I will
save.

Now, what an encouragement is this to faith! And
how, if rightly weighed and considered, would it dash
all the pleas of unbelief to pieces, and sweetly draw the
soul on to close with Christ in a marriage covenant!
For, pray, consider, what is the nature of a sovereign
grace and love? The nature of it is to act from itself to
itself, without any consideration of anything in us,
without respecting either the worthiness or the unworthiness of the creature at all. The nature of it is such
that it is neither constrained to, nor restrained from,
doing good to souls by anything either of good or evil
in them, but all runs freely. And, therefore, no matter
what I am, though never so vile and wretched in myself, I have to do with such love. And such love is the
spring of all Christ's dealings with me and carriages
towards me.

5.) The fifth gospel principle or encouragement
of faith which you should bear up yourself upon, and
dwell much in the contemplation of, is this: the great
design of Christ in all His undertakings for, and dis-
pensations towards, sinners is the illustrating and enthroning of His own grace. And the more vile, sinful,
and forlorn a wretch you are, the more will His grace
be enthroned and illustrated in your acceptance with
Him. Christ, in His dealings with and for sinners, not

only acts from a principle of sovereign grace, but in all
He carries on a design to enthrone that grace of His
and to make it glorious forever; yea, He acts, and will
act, suitably to such a design. "It is not what such and
such sinners do or do not deserve," says Christ, "that I
am to mind, but what My grace can do for them, and
what will make most for the glory of that grace, what
will set the brightest crown upon His head." This is evident from Ephesians 1:6, 12, and 14, which was
opened before upon another occasion.

Hence, those whom He saves, He saves in such a
way as may most lift up His own grace, His design
therein being "that grace might reign," as you have it,
Romans 5:21. Hence, you read of His justifying the un-
godly, Romans 4:5. He will have His grace triumph
over every soul whom He saves. Now, what an encouragement is this to faith! Christ not only sits upon a
throne of grace but also His design in dealing with
sinners is to set His grace upon the throne. Sinner, the
more vile and sinful you are, the more suitable it is to
Christ's design to save you. For the more vile and sinful
you are, the greater name and glory will His grace get
in your acceptatance and salvation by Him. The more
vile and sinful you are, the greater will be the declara-
tion of grace on Christ's part in your acceptance and
salvation. O! when Christ shall pardon a soul so guilty,
receive a soul so sinful, reconcile a soul that is such an
enemy as you are, how will this declare the glorious
riches of His grace in the view both of men and angels!
This will "show forth the exceeding riches of His
grace," as the expression is in Ephesians 2:7. And, the
more vile and sinful you are, the greater will be the
admiration of grace forever on your part. Where much

is forgiven, there will be the return of much love and much praise.

"O who am I?" says the soul, when once received to mercy, though more than ordinarily vile and sinful. "Who am I, that I should find grace in Christ's sight? What, such a rebel and then pardoned? Such an enemy, and yet reconciled? Such a black devil, and yet washed and made white in the blood of the Lamb? Such a fiend of hell and yet made a favorite of heaven? Such a filthy deformed wretch, and yet taken into the pure and lovely bosom of sweet Jesus! O grace, grace! How rich and free is grace!"

And O what praise and hallelujahs will there be tuned upon the tongues and spirits of such to God and the Lamb forever! When, therefore, you would go to Christ, and discouragements arise to keep you back from Him, you should dwell in the thoughts of, and bear up your soul upon, this consideration, reasoning thus with yourself: "True, I am a vile wretch, the chief of sinners, one on all accounts worthy to be abhorred and cast off by Christ. But what then? Christ acts towards sinners purely from a principle of grace and love. He regards neither worthiness nor unworthiness, whether a great sinner or a little sinner. It is all one to Him, as to His accepting of me. Moreover, His design is to crown His grace and render that glorious; and the more vile I am, the more that design of His will take in my acceptance and salvation. However vile, therefore, I am, I will cast myself upon Him and put in for an espousal with Him."

6.) The sixth gospel principle or encouragment of faith which you should bear up yourself upon and dwell much in the contemplation of is this: it is the

glory and perfection of Christ as Mediator to receive
sinners and to give out Himself to them when they
come to Him. This, if rightly weighted, will mightily
help faith and lift the poor soul over his discouragements into the bosom and embraces of Jesus Christ. To
understand it aright, you must know that Christ has a
twofold glory and perfection—the glory and perfection
of His person as He is the Son of God, and the glory
and perfection of His office as He is Mediator and
Head of the second covenant.

The glory and perfection of His person as the Son
of God is infinitely complete and full. It admits neither
of diminution nor augmentation, being unchangeably
the same forever. But the glory and perfection of His
office as Mediator, in a great measure, arises from His
receiving sinners and bestowing Himself and His grace
upon them when they come to Him. And the more
sinners He receives, and the more grace He gives out
to them, the greater His glory and perfection in this
respect is. And it may be truly said that Christ, in receiving and giving out grace to sinners when they come
to Him, increases the revenue of His own glory and
more and more completes and perfects Himself as
Head and Mediator. Hence the church is called "His
fullness," Ephesians 1:22-23, "God gave Him to be
Head over all things to the church, which is His body,
the fullness of Him that filleth all in all. "

Now, if the church is Christ's fulness, then the
more that it is filled and completed by His receiving
sinners to Himself, and giving out grace to them, the
more full and complete He Himself, as to His media-
tory honor and perfection, grows. Hence also saints are
said to be "the glory of Christ," 2 Corinthians 8:23. As

Christ alone is their glory, so they also are His glory. And how His glory? Not only because they do, or should actually, glorify Him, but also because He has received them and laid out His grace upon them, and it is His grace only that shines forth in them. Hence that observation of Calvin upon the place, "They that excel most in grace and holiness, they peculiarly are the glory of Christ; because they have nothing but by free gift from Christ." Hence also Christ tells us that He is glorified in them, John 17:10. And He says expressly that the Spirit shall glorify Him because He shall receive of his, and give it unto us, John 16:14. By all which it appears that it is the glory and perfection of Christ as Mediator to receive sinners coming to Him and to bestow Himself and His grace upon them.

In short, my beloved, all that ever Christ has done for, and is made of God to, poor sinners, all His acts and all His offices as Mediator, receive their ultimate perfection in their full influences on us and our salvation. And as Christ receives His name and denomination of a Savior from His relation to, and acting for, poor sinners to redeem and save them, so the perfection of this office, and these acts of His, lie in the full accomplishment of our salvation. And, indeed, they would all be but vain and weak acts should He not fully save us coming to Him. O what encouragement is here to faith! And how must unbelief sink and die before this consideration if rightly improved. "True," may the soul say, "I am vile, sinful, and unworthy, but it is the honor of Christ to receive me. It is His glory to bestow Himself and His grace upon me. It is His perfection as a Mediator to accept and save me and such as I am. And, therefore, why should I be discouraged? I will go to Him and cast myself upon Him." Thus, bear up your souls upon, and encourage your faith with, these gospel principles, which is greatly necessary and will not a little conduce to an espousal between Christ and you.

Chapter 11

Directions how to attain unto this sweet and blessed espousal continued

To continue the directions from the previous chapter as to how to attain this sweet and blessed espousal:

4. *Would you indeed be espoused to Christ? Then take heed of all jealousies of Him and prejudices against Him. Be ever sure to maintain right thoughts of Him.* One of the great designs of Satan, and one of the most cursed workings of unbelief, is to prejudice souls against Christ and fill them with hard jealous thoughts of Him; which, if they can prevail in, they infallibly keep the soul from closing with Him in a marriage covenant. If a woman has jealousies and hard thoughts of a man, and is filled with prejudices against him, she is never likely to enter into a marriage covenant with him. And no more will a soul close with Christ in a marriage covenant as long as he is filled with hard thoughts of Him, and prejudices against Him. Watch, therefore, against this. The devil, together with the unbelief of our own hearts, will frame up a thousand strange notions and representations of Christ in the soul, thereby to prejudice us against Christ; but take heed of all these, and be sure to maintain right thoughts and apprehensions of Him. Particularly here take only two things:

1.) Be sure to maintain honorable thoughts of His person. Look upon Him as a person of glory and as having all excellencies in Him. It is the work and nature of unbelief to darken and obscure the person of Christ, to make that appear vile and contemptible in the eye of the soul whereby it effectually strengthens itself within him. And, indeed, there is nothing more prevalent to keep the soul from Christ than an ignorance of, or prejudice against, His personal worth and excellencies. This is that which made the Jews so generally reject Him: "They saw no beauty in Him for which they should desire Him, nor did they discern form or comeliness in Him," and, therefore, rejected Him. They looked no further than the outward form, the veil of His flesh. They did not see His divine beauty and glory, and so despised Him. And, my beloved, unless we look within this veil and come to view and contemplate Him as a person of glory, we shall also reject Him to our eternal perdition. Pray observe, it is the person of Christ that puts worth and virtue in all His doings, all His sufferings, all His offices, and all His promises. It is the worth and excellency of His person that makes His blood so precious, His promises so sweet, His righteousness so glorious, His grace so efficacious, His love so endearing. It is the worth and excellency of His person that gives authority to all the commands of faith, and awes the heart to obedience; and it is the worth and excellency of His person that is one of the most powerful attractions to draw and allure the hearts of the sons of men to Him. If, therefore, His person is undervalued, if the glory and dignity of that is not seen, we are never likely to enter into a marriage covenant with Him. Therefore, soul, if ever you would be espoused to this Christ, always maintain honorable thoughts of His person. Behold His glory, as the glory of the only begotten of the Father, and beg Him more and more to reveal His personal worth and excellencies to you.

2.) Be sure always to maintain good thoughts of His ways, kingdom, and government. Admit not of one jealousy to Christ, as if He were a hard, severe Husband, as if He carried it with rigor and severity towards His spouses. If the devil and unbelief fail in their other attempts, then they endeavor to prejudice souls against Christ, persuading them that He is a hard Master, an austere Husband who rules with intolerable rigor and severity. "I knew," said he in the gospel, "that you were an austere man," Matthew 25:24. And hereby the soul is scared off from Christ. But, soul, if ever you would be espoused to Him, take heed of any such jealousies of Him, or prejudice against Him, keeping up good thoughts of Him and His ways, Him and His government, and be much in contemplating the sweetness both of Him and His ways.

Is He severe? Pray, wherein lies His severity? Does He call you to bear His yoke? He does, but it is an easy yoke. Does He enjoin you to bear His burden? He does, but it is a light burden: "My yoke is easy and My burden is light." Does He expect you should take up the cross? He does, but it is a sweet cross, a gainful cross, an honorable cross, a cross that is inlaid with love and overlaid with divine sweetness, a cross that has a crown annexed to it, even a crown of life, Revelation 2:10; a cross that has a crown here, for it is an honor to suffer for Christ, Acts 5:41. And it is a cross that will greaten and brighten our crown hereafter. "Blessed are ye when men shall revile you, and persecute you, for great is your reward in heaven." Does He call you to perform such and such services? He does, but withal He gives you strength to perform them, helping your infirmities by His good Spirit. And in case you fail and come short in what He calls for, what then? Why, then, He pities and spares you as a father does his son who serves him. He overlooks your failings and defects. Can you do nothing? You only have a mind to serve Him? Why, then, He accepts that willing mind according to what you have, and not according to what you have not. When you cannot pour out a prayer, a sigh or a groan is accepted by Him. Will you have the throne in you and rule in your souls? He will, but this way of rule is most sweet; for He rules with love and rewards with life. He gives a throne for a throne, a throne in glory for a throne in your souls. What shall I say? His ways are ways of pleasantness, and His paths are all peace. O what pleasure, what delight, what solace and satisfaction of soul, is there to be found in walking in them!

In a word, His whole service is perfect freedom, and there is no true freedom but in His ways and service. It is a great saying which I have read in one of the ancients, "Who would not reign? But would you reign happily? Serve King Jesus, and you shall reign, because to serve Him is true reigning." Thus you see there is no just reason for hard thoughts of Christ in this respect but rather the contrary. Accordingly answer and throw off all those black reproaches which the devil and unbelief cast upon this good Lord. And be sure to maintain good thought of Him and His ways, which will not a little conduce to the promoting of an espousal between Him and you.

5. *Would you indeed be espoused to Christ? Then study and contemplate much how infinitely grateful and acceptable Christ is.* Sinners know not (or, if they know, they consider not) who or what Christ is. They mind not how acceptable a good He is to souls and, therefore, they slight Him. "Had you known," says Christ to the woman, "the gift of God, and who it is that speaks to you, you would have asked Him, and He would have given you living water." Truly, if men knew Christ and His infinite acceptableness, they would run to Him and close with Him in a marriage covenant. Study, therefore, and contemplate this much, thereby possessing your soul with a deep sense of it. The Apostle, speaking but of one truth concerning Christ, tells us it is "worthy of all acceptance." And if so, what acceptance must Christ Himself, yea, Christ, with all His treasures, be worthy of? And how should our souls cleave to Him and take Him into our embraces? There are, among others, five things which speak a good to be eminently grateful and acceptable: worth and excellency, usefulness and serviceabless, suitableness and conveniency, sweetness and delight, durableness and unchangeableness in all. All these are found in Christ, who offers Himself and His love to us.

1.) There is worth and excellency in Christ, yea, incomparable worth and excellency. The Apostle speaks of an excelling excellency that there is in the knowledge of Christ, Philippians 3:8. Now, the knowledge of Christ is so excellent because Christ is excellent. Christ indeed is all worth, all excellency. He is an infinite ocean of beauty and glory. He is the chiefest among ten thousand and altogether lovely. All excellencies dwell in Him as in their proper fountain; and

they all meet and are united in Him as lines in their
proper center. Some beauty, some excellencies, you
find scattered up and down among the creatures—the
saints and angels, the sun, moon, and stars, and the
like—but alas! it is scattered, and it is scattered but
here and there a drop; but in Christ you have all
beauty, all worth, all excellency, in a blessed union and
conjunction. You have all in one, and that unchangeably. O what a portion is Christ! O that the saints
would dig deeper into the treasures of His wisdom and
excellencies! Truly it is sweet digging there, and there,
in some sort, there will be room for digging to all eternity. For even through eternity new wonders of glory
will arise, new beauties and excellencies will appear
and shine forth in Christ. What shall I say? He has in
Him all the excellencies of both worlds, and is indeed
deservedly the wonder of both. In Him there is a con-
fluence of all the lovely properties, the drawing attributes, the ravishing beauties, the bright, shining,
and glorious perfections of the infinitely blessed Deity.
Hence, says He, "all that the Father hath is Mine,"
which may be understood of His divine perfections.
Hence, also, He is said to be equal with God; that is,
whatever divine perfections there are in God the
Father are found in Christ. In Him is expressed the
whole person of the Father, the whole essence, being,
and beauty of the Father. And, as a learned man has
observed, "Christ the Son is in all things like the
Father, this only excepted, that He is not the person of
the Father. Hence also He is said to be the brightness
of His Father's glory, and the express image of His person." All the Father's glories and excellencies shine
forth in Him, and He perfectly represents the Father

to us. Thus, Christ is a person of excellency, and so most acceptable. And O who would not accept and embrace such a Christ? And how great a wickedness is it to reject Him? I cannot but here take up the complaint of a holy man, "O pity, pity forevermore," says he, "that there should be such a one as Christ Jesus; so boundless, so bottomless, so incomparable, so infinite an excellency and sweetness, and so few that will take Him. They miserably lose their love who will not bestow it upon this lovely one."

2.) There is usefulness and serviceableness in Christ. As Christ is a person of the highest excellency, so He is of the greatest and most absolute need, use, and service to poor souls. Indeed, He is the one needful good. Christ is so much needed by, and of so much use and service to, poor souls that they cannot possibly do well and be happy without Him. Pray consider, we provoke God and He is angry with us, and by Christ alone it is that we receive the atonement. We sin and load ourselves with guilt, and by Christ alone it is that we are or can be discharged from it. "In Him have we redemption through His blood, even the forgiveness of sins." We have a hard and impenitent heart, a heart that cannot repent, and by Christ, and Christ alone, it is that we can obtain repentance, He being exalted to give repentance unto Israel, as well as remission of sins. We are at a dreadful distance from God, "afar off," as the Scripture speaks, and by Christ and Him alone it is that "we are made nigh."

The best of saints as well as the worst of sinners have an absolute need of Christ, and He is of daily use and service to them. Nor can they live one day or one hour without Him. Indeed, He is their life, and without

Him, therefore, they are dead and undone as well as others. Without Him they can do nothing. Without Him every duty will be too hard, every burden will be too heavy, every temptation will be too strong, every lust will be too mighty for them. Without Him they would yet fall short of the eternal rest and would make shipwreck of faith, souls, and all forever. Without Him, neither saints nor sinners can have any access to God, any intercourse or communion with Him, in which, notwithstanding, the whole of our happiness lies. "I am the way, and no man cometh to the Father but by Me," John 14:6. "And through Him," said the Apostle, "we have access unto the Father by one Spirit," Ephesians 2:18. Without Him we could have no peace with God, for He alone is our peace. And having peace with God, without Him we could not maintain our peace one hour, it being He alone who is our Advocate and propitiation with the Father. Thus, He is every way most needful and most useful to eternal souls. O how grateful, how acceptable then is He, and ought He to be to us!

3.) There is suitableness and conveniency also in Christ to the souls of men. The suitableness and conveniency of any good renders it acceptable to us. How acceptable is bread to a hungry man because it is a good suitable to him! How acceptable is drink to a thirsty man because it is a good suitable to him! Now, there is an admirable sweetness and conveniency in Christ to the souls of men, and that in all the cases of them. Why, then, should He not be acceptable to them? We are sick, and sick to death, and Christ is a Physician. And what more suitable to the sick than a physician? We are sinful, and sinful to damnation. We are lost sinners and Christ is a Savior. And who or what is more suitable to lost sinners that a Saviour? e are poor captives, captives of sin and Satan, in bondage to death and the curse, and Christ is a Redeemer. And who or what is more suitable to captives than a Redeemer? We are under the tyranny and usurpation of many mighty, powerful lusts, lusts that are imposing upon us every hour, and we are no ways able to deal with them. But Christ is a great and powerful King who can subdue all, and whose arrows shall be sharp in the hearts of all His and our enemies. And what more suitable to persons in such a circumstance than such a King? We are dead and Christ is life; and what more suitable for the dead than life? We are poor and miserable, and Christ is gold to enrich us. Are we naked? Christ is clothing for us. Are we blind? He is eye-salve for us. Are we in prison? He is liberty. Are we hungry? He is bread. Are we thirsty? He is the water of life which those that drink of shall never thirst. Are we troubled? He is rest. Are we drooping and desponding? He is the Consolation of Israel. Are we bewildered? He is a guide. Are we borne down in our spiritual conflicts? He is the Captain of our salvation who will fight for us. O how suitable in every way is Christ to souls! And being so suitable, why should He not be acceptable to us. Poor sinner! Is there any in heaven or earth who will so suit and answer the various wants and cases of your soul as Christ does and will? Why, then, should you not account Him worthy of all acceptance?

4.) There is a sweetness and delight in Christ. Everyone is drawn and allured by pleasure and delight. What is it that makes sin, that cursed thing sin, pleasing and grateful to so many? Surely one great thing is that pleasure and delight which they find, at least promise themselves to find, in it. And indeed generally, the more sweet and delightful things are, the more readily and greedily they are embraced by the sons of men. Why, then, should not Christ be grateful and acceptable to us? Is there any so sweet, so pleasant, so delightful, as He? He is a fountain of sweetness as well as excellency. Experienced souls will tell you that there is more sweetness in one descent of love from Christ than in all the delights of sin and the creature. This is that which sweetens the sharpest affliction; yea, this is that, and that alone, which sweetens death itself and enables the soul truly to triumph over it. O the sweet bathing that there is in the fountain of Christ's love! How sweet are His fruits! "I sat down under His shadow, says the spouse, with sweet delight, and His fruits were sweet to my taste." By fruits, I understand the purchase of His blood and the effect of His love: peace, pardon, righteousness, justification, sanctification and holiness, acceptance with God, and the like. And O how sweet are these! How pleasant are these! With what solace and satisfaction may a believing soul feed and feast Himself upon these! How sweet is His presence—intercourse, and communion with Him! This made the spouse to be glad, and rejoice in Him. This, indeed, sets the soul down at the very gate of heaven, where He says "it is good to be here." And, indeed, who is there that knows what communion with Christ means who does not find an incomparable sweetness, solace, and satisfaction in it? This is that which fills some with joy unspeakable and full of glory even here; and this is that which will be the joy and delight of heaven forever. In every way, Christ is every field of pleasure, a very paradise of joy, and a very fountain of delight. O why, then, should He not be more grateful and acceptable to us?

5.) There is durableness and unchangeableness in Christ, which, being added to all the former, renders Him even infinitely the more grateful and acceptable. Possibly some worth, some usefulness, some suitableness, some sweetness and delight may be found in the creature and creature enjoyments. But alas! this allays the acceptableness of all, that it is fading, dying, and changing. And, indeed, whatever is short and but for a season cannot challenge any great acceptance. But now Christ is lasting, durable, and unchangeable. He is the same yesterday, today, and forever. What He was He is, and what He is He always will be. He was most excellent, most useful, most suitable, most sweet and delightful to souls, and so He is and always will be. He is immutable. He changes all things, but is Himself unchangeable—never new, never old. Hence also Christ Himself tells us that He is the Alpha and Omega, He that was and is and is to come. He is ever the same in love, in beauty, in fullness, in faithfulness, and in all desirablenesses. And O how grateful and acceptable does this render Him! All our enjoyments here below fade and change. Yea, we ourselves change; "changes and war are upon us," as Job speaks; yea, some of us are daily waiting for our great and last change. But O! blessed be God. Christ fades not. Christ changes not. What He was to, and what He has done for, souls formerly, that He is to, and that He can be for, souls now. Yea, and that He will be to, and will be able to do for, souls hereafter. For He is still to come as He was, and is, and so is to come, which is a sweet word.

Poor soul, hitherto it may be you have gone through your work and warfare with some comfort and courage, but that which dampens and terrifies you is the apprehension of what may be to come. "O," you say, "the trials that are to come, the difficulties that are to come, the temptations that are to come, the storms and tempests that are to come!" Well, soul, for your encouragement under all know that whatever is to come, Christ is to come too. Are there trials to come? Christ is to come too. Are there difficulties and temptations to come? Christ is to come too. Are there storms and tempests to come? Christ is to come too. And while Christ is to come, fear not; only close with Him in a marriage covenant and make Him yours. Then come what will come, come what can come, all will be well. Thus Christ is every way acceptable and infinitely acceptable. And as ever, soul, you would be indeed espoused to Him, dwell much in the study and contemplation of His acceptableness. Labor to be possessed with a deep and daily renewed sense of it, which will sweetly draw and allure your soul to Him.

6. *Would you indeed be espoused to Christ? Then be sure that you pitch your faith aright upon Him, and close effectually with Him in a way of believing.* It is faith that is both the great uniting and the great interesting grace. It unites us to Christ and interests us in Christ. It is that, as has been formerly declared and evidenced, which puts Christ and the soul into the bosom and embraces of each other's love and by which the marriage knot is tied between them. If ever, therefore, you would be indeed espoused unto Him, look well to your faith. See

that you pitch that aright upon Him, closing with Him and embracing Him—not by halves but thoroughly; not feignedly but intimately and cordially.

But here some may say, "How may we pitch our faith aright upon Christ so as to get conjugal union and communion with Him?" Three things must be done in order hereunto, which I desire you to look well to:

     1.) See that you wholly quit and renounce yourselves. Self and believing are at the utmost distance from and enmity with each other that is imaginable. They are irreconcilably opposite to each other. And where faith takes place, there self vanishes and dies away, and that in all its notions and with all its accomplishments. Hence, says Christ, "If any man will come after Me," believe on me, be espoused to Me, "let him deny himself," renounce himself, go out of himself; let self become nothing with him. And, indeed, the soul that believes in Christ does go quite out of himself. He sees and feels himself to be a poor, empty nothing in all respects. He sees and finds his strength to be weakness, his wisdom folly, his beauty blackness, his righteousness sin, his all nothing. And thus must we, if ever we would indeed believe and get union with Christ. O my beloved, one of the great things which stands between faith and us, Christ and us, is self! This, indeed, is the soul's darling, the firstborn, as one calls it, of his love and delights, and he is loath to part with it. But part with it he must, and renounce it he must, or he can never believe aright, nor is he ever likely to have any part or lot in Christ. Every step out of self is a step towards Christ and faith in Christ. And we must be divorced from the one if ever we are to be married to the other. Particularly, you must quit and renounce self, especially in this threefold notion: self-will, self-worth, self-interest.

You must quit and renounce self-will. He that indeed believes must, in a sort, have no will of His own, but His will must be wholly melted or resigned up into the will of Christ; hence the church is said to be subject unto Christ, Ephesians 5:24. We are apt to live in our own wills, and are exceedingly fond of and set upon having our wills, however cross and contrary they are to the will of Christ. But if ever we would believe so as to get union with Christ, our stubborn wills must bow. Our proud wills must bow down, and must, in all things as much as possible, be referred and resigned into Christ's will. And with good reason, for His will is the rule of goodness as well as the first cause of all things. We must not think to say we are lords, but must bow to Christ as the great and only Lord.

You must quit and renounce self-worth and self-righteousness. You must renounce all worth and righteousness of your own in point of justification and acceptance with God. It is a great word which I shall speak. Men's duties, living under the gospel, keep almost as many from Christ and believing as their sins do. My meaning is this: As the love of sins keeps some, so confidence in duties, a confidence in self-worth, self-righteousness, keeps multitudes of others from Christ and believing. And the truth is, my beloved, this piece of self is the great idol of the soul, and that which men are marvellously loath to quit and renounce. And, indeed, it is oftentimes so painted and, as it were, so spiritualized, acted with so much state and set out with so many ornaments, that it would make anyone be in love with it. But yet this idol, so dear as it is to the soul, must be denied and renounced. This darling must be cast off, and that with loathing and abomination, in respect of soul saving, if ever you would believe and be united to Christ. And the soul that indeed believes looks upon himself to be the poorest, most despicable and undone creature in the world, notwithstanding all. He throws away not only his rags but his robes too—all his privileges, all his performances, all his moral excellencies and attainments, as to a dependence upon them for life and salvation. This Paul did, Philippians 3:8-9, of which more hereafter.

The soul's language in the work of believing is such as this: I am a poor, vile, empty, nothing in myself. I am nothing, I can do nothing, and I deserve nothing. I am nothing but sin. I can do nothing but offend and provoke God, and I deserve nothing but frowns and death from Him. If ever I am saved, it is free grace must save me. If ever I find favor in God's sight, it must be purely from grace in Christ. Alas! I have walked contrary to God all my days. My heart and life both have been full of enmity and provocation against Him, and my very duties are damning, my best righteousness being as filthy rags, Isaiah 64:6. And indeed, till it comes to this with us, we are likely to remain strangers to Christ and faith in Christ. I shall only say this further as to this particular that no men in the world are further off from Christ and union with Him through believing than such as trust in their own worth, in their own righteousness. Christ Himself tells us that publicans and harlots enter the kingdom of heaven before such.

You must quit and renounce self-interest. That is to

say, you must be at a parting point with all. You must be willing to forego all your outward interests and concerns for Christ when He calls you to it, thinking nothing too much or too good for Him. This Christ expresses in Matthew 10:37, "He that loveth father or mother more than Me is not worthy of Me; and He that loveth son or daughter more than Me is not worthy of Me." And again, Luke 14:33, "Whosoever he be of you that forsaketh not all that he hath, he cannot be My disciple." In a word, the meaning is not that all who come to Christ must actually forsake all those things and deny themselves as to the enjoyment of them; but the meaning is, first, that we must have a very diminutive love for these in comparison of Christ; and, second, that we must be at a parting point with all for Christ's sake and at Christ's call. And truly, it is but reasonable that we should be so. He who actually parted with so much for us highly deserves that we should be in a readiness to part with our little all for Him. Thus, we must wholly quit and renounce ourselves if we would indeed believe and have union with Christ.

2.) Would you pitch your faith aright upon Christ and be indeed espoused to Him? Then labor to get a right notion and apprehension of Him as the great Object of faith. One great reason why many fail and miscarry in their faith, and so fall short of Christ, is their ignorance of Him. They do not have a right notion and apprehension of Christ as the great Object of faith. And, indeed, unless Christ is rightly known and apprehended by us, we are never likely to pitch our faith aright upon Him. "How shall they believe," says the Apostle, "in Him of whom they have not heard?"

Romans 10:14. How shall they believe? That is, men cannot believe aright on one who has not been revealed and made known to them. A blind, ignorant, faith is never likely to reach union and communion with Christ. And, my beloved, if we would believe aright on Christ, we must know Him aright and apprehend Him aright.

Faith, in Scripture, is sometimes expressed by knowledge. Not that knowledge alone is all that is requisite to faith, but it notes this much to us, that the knowledge of Christ is such a requisite to believing, that there can be no true believing without it. Hence also Christ spoke of "seeing the Son, and believing on Him"; seeing before believing, and seeing in order to believing. "This is the will of Him that sent Me, that whosoever seeth the Son and believeth on Him shall have everlasting life." By "seeing the Son," here we are to understand the true knowledge of Christ. Hence also, they who come to Christ and believe savingly on Him are said, in order thereunto, to be taught of God, and to have heard and learned of the Father. And, pray, what have they been taught of God? What have they learned of Him but the knowledge of Christ as the great Object of faith? At least, this is one great lesson which all who believe do and must learn. As ever, therefore, you would pitch your faith aright upon Christ, labor to know and apprehend Him as He is revealed and offered in the gospel.

How we are to view and apprehend Christ

1. *View and apprehend Him in His Godhead and divine nature.* The gospel reveals Him in His divinity. It propounds Him to our faith as God, the true God, the great God, the mighty God, God over all. And thus should faith eye and apprehend Him. Thus Thomas's faith apprehended Him when he said, "My Lord and my God." Indeed, nothing but a Godhead—an infinite, eternal, unchangeable Godhead—is a foundation strong enough for faith to build upon.

2. *View and apprehend Him in His personal relation, not only as God, but also as God the Son, and so as distinguished from the Father.* Thus, the gospel reveals and propounds Him to our faith, and thus also should our faith view and apprehend Him. Thus Peter's faith, with the rest in whose name he spoke, eyed and apprehended Him, John 6:69: "We believe and are sure, that Thou art that Christ, the Son of the living God." There is a distinct honor due to every person in the sacred Trinity. And the more distinctly our faith eyes and apprehends Christ in His personal relation as Son, the more complete it is and the more it gives Him the honor of that relation.

3. *View and apprehend Him in His humanity, or as the Son of God incarnate.* The gospel reveals and propounds Christ as the object of faith to us, not simply as God, and as God the Son, but as God the Son incarnate, as the Word made flesh, John 1:14; or, as God manifested in the flesh, 1 Timothy 3:16; as having taken human nature into personal union with Himself, and so being both God and man in one person. And thus also should faith eye and apprehend Him. "You believe in

God," says He, "believe also in Me," John 14:1. Hence also He speaks so often of eating His flesh and drinking His blood, of giving His flesh for the life of the world. And withal He tells us that His flesh is meat indeed and His blood is drink indeed. By all which He signifies to us that our faith must respect and apprehend Him as man as well as God, as the Son incarnate: and indeed, thus He is the next and most immediate Object of faith. The Godhead or Divinity is the ultimate Object of faith, but Christ the Son incarnate is the next and most immediate Object of faith. Hence we are said by Him to believe in God. Faith first eyes Christ as man, or the Son incarnate, and by Him comes ultimately to focus itself upon God. The humanity is a gate to the Divinity, that by which our faith passes to the Godhead. "And," as a great divine speaks, "he that comes not to Christ as man shall never come to Him as God." The truth is, faith cannot deal with God immediately but as God clothed with our nature.

4. *View and apprehend Him in His office of mediatorship.* The gospel reveals and propounds Christ to our faith in His office. It propounds and reveals Him as Christ, as the true Messiah and Savior of the world, as one sealed, sent, and anointed by the Father for the redemption of lost souls. And thus also should faith eye and apprehend Him. So also did Peter's faith apprehend Him: "Thou art the Christ," said he, "the Son of the living God." Hence we read of "believing that Jesus is the Christ." Hence also Christ tells the Jews, "If ye believe not that I am He, ye shall die in your sins." "If ye believe not that I am He," that is, the Messiah, the Christ, the Savior that was promised. O! faith is short of that notion it should have of Christ unless it thus

eyes Him in His office.

5. *View Him and apprehend Him in His infinite ability and sufficiency for the discharge of His office.* The gospel reveals and propounds Him to our faith as one able to save to the very uttermost. And accordingly should our faith eye and apprehend Him. It reveals Him indeed both as an only and all-sufficient Savior. As an only Savior: "Look unto Me and be saved, all ye ends of the earth; for I am God, and there is none besides Me," Isaiah 45:22. "Neither is there salvation in any other; nor is there any other name given under heaven, whereby we may be saved, but His only," Acts 4:12. And as an all-sufficient Savior: "My flesh is meat indeed, and My blood is drink indeed, and He that eateth Me, even He shall live by Me." It reveals Him in the infinite virtue of His blood, the inexhaustible fullness of His grace, the completeness of His obedience, the excellency of His righteousness, the perfection of His satisfaction, and the like. And thus should our faith eye and apprehend Him. O labor for such a notion and apprehension of Christ as this is, if ever you would believe aright, and be indeed espoused to Christ! Labor for a sound, clear, distinct knowledge of Him as the great object of faith. Pray much for a spirit of wisdom and revelation in the knowledge of Him. That was the Apostle's prayer for the Ephesians, and let it be yours for yourselves.

3.) Would you pitch your faith aright upon Christ and be indeed espoused to Him? Then be sure to make a right choice or election of Him, being thus known and apprehended. To have a right notion and apprehension of Christ is good and necessary in order

to union with Him by believing, but it is not enough.
Know that Christ, being known and apprehended,
must also be chosen and embraced by us, and that as
He is offered in the gospel. To know and apprehend
Christ is an act of the mind or understanding, but to
choose and embrace Christ is an act of the will and affections. And though faith has its rise and origin in the
mind, yet it has its completion and perfection in the
will and affections—these liking, choosing, and embracing Him, and that in a way suitable to what the
mind sees and apprehends concerning Him. And this
must be added to the former or there is no believing,
and so no conjugal union and communion with Christ.
Hence that saying of the Apostle, "With the heart man
believeth unto righteousness," Romans 10:10. True believing, then, is with the heart.

Now, by the heart here, as elsewhere in Scripture, is
meant the will and affections. Accordingly, to believe
with the heart is for the will and affections to choose
and embrace Christ as He is revealed and offered in
the gospel. This is called receiving Christ, John 1:12.
We receive Christ into our wills when we choose Him
and adhere to Him for life and salvation. And we receive Him into our affections when we love Him, desire
Him, and delight in Him. And this is believing. "To believe," says Calvin, "is nothing else but to choose and
embrace Christ with a sincere affection of mind as He
is revealed and offered in the gospel." And this, indeed, is the great vital act of faith, and that whereby
our conjugal union and communion with Christ is
more especially brought about. This is that which
makes Christ ours and puts us into the possession of
Him. "Mary," says Christ, "has chosen the better part,

which shall never be taken from her." She had chosen
Christ, and her choice of Him had made Him her own,
and so her own that she could never lose Him, never
be deprived of Him. Indeed, a right choice of Christ
makes Him ours. It unites us to Him and interests us in
Him forever. A little further to help you in this business, know that a right choice of Christ is accomplished by these three steps.

(1) The soul, apprehending Christ as before, likes Him and approves of Him as the best and
most suitable Savior, the most lovely and desirable
Object in heaven or earth. The soul says of Christ, as
was said of the land of Canaan, "The land is an exceeding good land." So this Christ, says the soul, is an exceeding good Christ. This Savior is an exceeding good
Savior. There is none like Him, there is no beauty like
His beauty, no blood like His blood, no fullness like
His fullness, no love like His love.

(2) The soul desires Him and longs after
Him, and that with a strong, ardent, and vigorous affection. This is called "hungering and thirsting after
Christ." The soul, seeing Christ and approving of Him,
longingly cries out, "O a Christ! a Christ! O that this
good Christ were mine!"

(3) The soul is, by grace, sweetly and powerfully determined upon Christ so as actually to make a
solemn and deliberate choice of Him, singling Him
out from all other things in heaven and earth as the
best and most desirable good and most worthy of His
dearest and most intimate embraces. The soul now
pitches its choice upon Christ to be its Head and
Husband, its Lord and Savior, its rest, its treasure, its
happiness, its all forever.

Now, by these steps, see that you come to make a
right choice of Christ. Be sure that you like Him and
approve of Him as the best and most desirable Object
in heaven or earth. Truly, if you view Him aright, you
cannot but like Him and approve of Him as such. See
that the desire of your souls is indeed towards Him
above all others. View Him till you fall in love with
Him, yea, till you fall sick of love for Him. And be sure
not to rest till you get your will sweetly and powerfully
determined upon Him so as to make a free, solemn,
deliberate choice of Him, passing by all other lovers
and taking Him alone into the bosom and embraces of
your faith and love.

Rules to Make a Right Choice of Christ

Now, that you may be sure to make a right choice
of Christ, such a choice of Christ as may keep Him
yours, and tie the marriage knot between Him and
you, observe herein these six great rules:

1. *Be sure that you choose and embrace Christ Himself,
and not someone else instead of Him.* It is a great and
awakening saying which a worthy divine has: "Many
now take Christ by guess; but be sure that it is He, and
only He, whom you embrace. His sweet smell, His
lovely voice, His face, His gracious working in the soul,
will soon tell if it is He or not." So, I say, be sure that it
is He. Many mistake the object. They close with something else instead of Christ. At best they choose
Christ's portion, His benefits, His privileges, His purchases, but not His person. But my advice to you is,
pitch on nothing short of the person of Christ. Then is
our faith, beyond all doubt, rightly pitched upon

Christ—when Christ Himself, not His benefits and privileges only, is chosen and embraced by us. A marriage, if right, is between person and person, not between person and portion or person and estate, that being a resulting thing. So here, in this spiritual marriage, faith does not marry the soul to the portion, benefits, privileges, and purchases of Christ but to Christ Himself. True, I do not deny, first, but that true faith gives the soul an interest in all the benefits, privileges, and purchases of Christ. Nor, second, do I say that the soul may not have an eye and respect to these in his choice and closing with Christ. Yea, usually these are the first things that faith has in its eye. The first thing the soul usually looks at and is taken with when he is drawn to Christ is that peace, that pardon, that righteousness, that deliverance from sin, death, and hell which he sees is found and treasured up in Christ for souls. But, though these things are so, yet the soul does and must go higher. He must look at and pitch upon the person of Christ or his faith is not as right and complete as it ought to be. Alas! it is the person of Christ that is the great fountain of all grace and all manifestations of God to us, and faith, accordingly, closes in with His person. The spouse's faith seems so to do, Song of Solomon 5:10. She had her eye upon the personal beauty and glory of Christ and, accordingly, embraced Him with her faith and love. Hence also you have so often those expressions: "I sought Him whom my soul loved," and, "Saw you Him whom my soul loveth?" Her love, and so her faith, was fixed upon Christ Himself. And thus you fix your faith and love upon Him. So shall you be sure not to miss of a conjugal union and communion with Him.

2. *Be sure that you choose a whole Christ and not a part of Him only.* My meaning is, see that you choose and embrace Christ in all His offices, as a King as well as a Priest and a Lord as well as a Savior. And, as in all His offices, so for all those ends and uses for which God has designed Him and the gospel revealed Him to us—for holiness as well as righteousness, for sanctification as well as justification. I need not tell you that Christ is a King as well as a Savior, and that as such He is revealed and offered in the gospel to our faith: "Him hath God exalted a Prince and a Savior, to give repentance unto Israel, and remission of sins." And they who will have Him as a Savior to give them pardon must have Him as a Prince to give them repentance. Christ's rest and His yoke go together in the gospel offer, Matthew 11:28-29. Nor need I tell you that God has appointed Him, and the gospel reveals Him, to be our sanctification as well as our justification. So you have it expressly in 1 Corinthians 1:30. Accordingly, then, we choose Christ and embrace Him aright when we choose and embrace Him under each notion; when we choose and embrace Him not as a Savior only but as a Lord too; not only as a Priest to procure pardon and reconciliation for us but also as a Prince to rule, govern, and command us; not only as our righteousness to justify us but as a fountain of grace to make us holy. And thus true faith chooses and embraces Him, Isaiah 45:24: "Surely shall one say, in the Lord I have righteousness and strength." Mark, faith chooses Christ not only for righteousness but for strength too; righteousness for justification, and strength for holiness and sanctification. Christ's language to the soul in the offer of Himself is such as this: "Poor soul, you are in a dead,

lost, undone condition. God is angry with you, hell
gapes for you, justice calls loud for vengeance against
you, and there is no hope, no help, no salva-tion for
you but in and by Me and union with Me. And lo! I am
willing to bestow Myself, with all My fullness, upon you.
But remember this, I will rule and command you. If I
am your Savior, I will be your Lord and King too. If you
will share in My redemption, you shall be content to
bear My yoke, to bow to My scepter, to submit to My
laws and kingdom."

Accordingly, faith's answer, if right, is this: "I consent, Lord. It is but fit that He who saves should rule
and reign, that He who redeems should rule and reign;
that He who redeems should be bowed and submitted
to. I willingly give up myself to Thy holy and spiritual
government. Thy yoke is easy, Thy scepter is righteous,
Thy kingdom is full of peace and joy, and I desire to
come under them. I would have Thee to make me holy
as well as righteous, to subdue this rebellious heart of
mine and to rule in me by Thy pure Spirit as well as to
save me by Thy perfect obedience." O see that you thus
choose and embrace a whole Christ, else your faith is
not aright, nor are you likely to attain unto a conjugal
union and communion with Him.

3. *Be sure that you choose Christ singly and alone, and
not join something else with Him.* Some are for com-
pounding with Christ. They would join someone else
in partnership with Him. But as Christ must not be di-
vided, so neither will He be compounded. He will be
all or nothing at all to souls, and so true faith closes
with Him. Hence, with the new creature, Christ is said
to be all and in all. The patriarchs, as one observes,
had, many of them, a wife and concubine; but it is not

so here. No, as faith chooses a whole Christ, so it chooses Christ singly and alone without joining anything else in partnership with Him. It matches the soul to Christ with an absolute exclusion of all other matches. Indeed, faith sees enough in a single Christ without the help of anything else, and, accordingly, chooses and embraces Him. And so must your faith choose and embrace Him or you are likely to miss conjugal union and communion with Him, especially in the great business of acceptatance with God.

Some would fain compound with Christ in this business. They would have Christ but they would have their own duties too. They would have His righteousness but they would have their own righteousness too. They would have theirs bear a share with His in point of righteousness and justification before God. 'Tis Calvin's observation that the foundation of our first step towards our obtaining an interest in the righteousness of God is for a man to renounce and go out of his own righteousness. Thus I am sure Paul's faith chose and embraced Christ, "Those things which were gain to me, those I counted loss for Christ; yea, doubtless, and I count all things but loss for the excellency of the knowledge of Christ Jesus my Lord; for whom I have suffered the loss of all things, and count them but dung, that I may win Christ and be found in Him; not having mine own righteousness, which is of the law, but that which is through the faith of Christ, the righteousness which is of God by faith."

Pray, mark his faith here. He chooses and embraces Christ for his righteousness and justification, and herein he joins nothing with Him. He pitches singly and nakedly upon Christ alone, renouncing all other things whatever. He had as much of his own to have leaned and depended upon, in this point, as any mere man that ever lived since sin entered the world; for in privileges, in graces, in services, and in sufferings for Christ (I am apt to think), he excelled all mere men. But yet he rests on none of these. No, nor so much as joins anything of it with Christ but rejects and renounces all—and that with the greatest loathing and detestation in the point of justification, cleaving singly and nakedly to Christ alone. Says he, "I count all but loss, yea, dung"; that is, as the most vile and loathsome thing, and I would not be found in it for a thousand worlds.

The truth is, to join anything of our own with Christ in this business is what excludes us from any share in Christ or any benefit by Christ. So much the Apostle expresses in Galatians 5:2-4: "Behold, I Paul say unto you, that if ye be circumcised, Christ shall profit you nothing. For I testify again to every man that is circumcised, that he is a debtor to do the whole law. Christ is become of no effect unto you, whosoever of you are justified by the law; ye are fallen from grace." The sum of the Apostle's design is to show that to join anything of our own with Christ in the business of righteousness and justification and not rest purely and entirely upon Him is what shuts us out from any part and lot in Christ, or any benefit and advantage by Him. For pray observe, there were among the Galatians some who joined the law with Christ, preferring and taking up circumcision as a part of that righteousness whereby they expected to be justified and saved. They were not so gross in their minds, as that great divine there observes, as to expect salvation merely by the observance of the law and their own obedience, but they were for sharing the business between this and Christ.

Now, what does Paul say to them? And by what does he labor to antidote the believers among them against this great error? Why, first, he tells them plainly that if they will join either circumcision or anything else of their own with Christ in this matter, then Christ shall profit them nothing, verse 2. And he asserts the same thing, verse 4, "Christ is become of no effect to you." That is, you shall have no part in Christ, no benefit by Christ. Christ is of no use, no benefit, no advantage, to you, any more than if He had never been. And indeed, as one observes upon that place, "Whoever is but for a half Christ in this business loses all of Christ."

Second, he tells them that if they will have anything of their own to bear a share with Christ in the matter of their salvation, they are debtors to do the whole law. If they will have their obedience to the law to have any share in their acceptance with God, then they must keep the whole law, for else all were nothing. It is a great speech of a learned interpreter upon these words: "Whoever is a debtor to do the whole law can never escape death, because he will always remain under guilt; for no one will ever be found who will be able to fulfill or satisfy the law. Such an obligation, therefore, is the certain damnation of the man that lies under it." Thus you see there must be nothing else of our own joined with Christ in the matter of our righteousness and justification with God, but our faith must cleave singly and nakedly to Christ alone.

The truth is, Christ's righteousness alone is sufficient to save and justify the worst of sinners. It is the righteousness of God and the righteousness of the law;

righteousness every way adequate and commensurate
to the strictest demands of law and justice; a righteousness as long, as broad, as deep, as high, as the sin
and guilt of the most scarlet, crimson sinners can be.
And why should any think of joining anything there-
with? Truly, to do so is to reflect great dishonor upon
it, and upon the wisdom and grace of God in ordering
it for our justification and salvation. And as we must
join nothing with Christ in the matter of righteousness
and justification, so neither must we join anything with
Him in the matter of our sanctification and holiness.
We should look for no grace, no holiness, but what
comes from Him and is wrought in us by Him. Nor,
indeed, will God own anything for grace and holiness
in us at last that does not come from Him. In all respects, therefore, let the language of your souls be, "O
none but Christ, none but Christ!"

4. *Be sure that you choose Christ and embrace Him as
your rest and happiness, and not only as one who is to bring
you unto rest and happiness.* Christ, my beloved, is not
only the way and means to bring men unto happiness,
but He also is *Himself* their happiness. And as such He
is offered to us, and should be chosen and embraced
by us. "I am the Way, the Truth, and the Life," that is,
as one glosses upon it, "I am the beginning, the
progress, and perfection of a Christian's happiness."
Sure I am, as Christ considered as the way is the means,
and what leads us into happiness, so Christ considered
as the life is Himself our happiness, our supreme happiness. And indeed, we come to Christ as the life by
Christ as the way. Sweet is that saying which I have read
in one of the ancients on this place: "We, your people,"
says he, speaking to Christ, "do come by Thee, to Thee,

because Thou art the Way, the Truth, and the Life—
the Way in Thy example, the Truth in Thy promise,
the Life in Thy reward."

"I am the Way, the Truth, and the Life," that is, as
another expounds it, "I am the only right way, the
supreme truth, the true life, the blessed life, the uncre-
ated life." And suitable hereunto is Calvin's observation upon these words: "The sum of this sentence is
this: He, whoever he is, that obtains and possesses
Christ can want nothing. Whoever therefore is not
content with Him alone aspires after something beyond the ultimate and highest perfection." And then
he concludes thus, "If anyone turns aside from Christ,
he can do nothing but err; if any one does not rest in
Him, he elsewhere feeds upon nothing but wind and
vanity; if anyone makes out after anything beyond
Him, he will find death instead of life."

O there are infinite beauties, delights, and perfections in Christ whereby He is able to fill and satisfy us
and make us happy! And, for my own part, as I desire
never to be happy if Christ is not able to bring me
happiness, so I desire no greater or better happiness
than what Christ is or can be to me. O there is all in
Him, all to fill, all to comfort, all to delight and ravish,
all to solace and satisfy the largest faculties of eternal
souls! "May I have but Christ," says Rutherford, "I shall
think myself as well heavened as any whatsoever." Truly
He and He alone is the quieting, resting, center of the
soul. Indeed, He, in His presence and our enjoyment
of Him, is heaven and happiness. It is the highest happiness which Christ promises His people here, and it is
the highest happiness which His people reckon upon
or hope for hereafter. Answerable whereunto is the

observation of one upon those words of Christ to the
thief upon the cross, Luke 23:43: "This day thou shalt
be with Me in paradise."

"With Me," says He. O wonderful goodness! He
does not say simply, "You shall be in paradise," or "you
shall be with angels," but "you shall be with Me. You
shall be satisfied with Him whom you desire."

Thus Christ is the rest and supreme happiness of
souls. And accordingly our faith should choose and
embrace Him. I will not say there is not true faith
where the soul does not come up to such a choice of
Christ as this; but this I will say, that though faith at
first may not thus choose Christ, yet afterwards, as it
grows upwards towards perfection, it comes to choose
Christ under this notion. And the more distinct it is in
choosing Christ as the supreme rest and happiness of
the soul, the more complete and perfect it is. Faith's
language to Christ, when it comes to maturity, is such
as this: "Lord, as all my life is in Thy death, all my healing in Thy wounds, all my righteousness in Thy obedience, so all my happiness is in Thy presence, all my
heaven in the bosom and embraces of Thy love. Nor
have I any in heaven but Thee; neither is there any
upon earth that I desire besides Thee." O, thus choose
Christ! Choose Him as the rest, the solace, the happiness of your souls, and never think of anything else to
be the least part of your happiness besides Christ.

5. *Be sure that you choose and embrace Christ with His
cross, and not only Christ with His crown; Christ crucified as
well as Christ glorified; Christ upon terms of suffering for
Him as well as reigning with Him, He calling thereunto.*
Thus also Christ offers Himself unto us, and thus must
He be chosen and embraced by us. "If any man will

come after Me, let Him deny himself, take up his cross, and follow Me." And "Whosoever doth not bear his cross, and come after Me cannot be My disciple." Some are for Christ and His crown, but they stick at His cross. They are for a reigning Christ but not for a persecuted Christ. But, my beloved, if you would so choose Him as to be married to Him, you must choose Him as upon the cross crucified as well as upon the throne glorified. The meaning is, you must choose Him with a firm resolution to suffer for Him if He calls you thereunto. You must choose Him as one persecuted and distressed upon earth as well as one dignified and glorified in heaven. In a word, you must choose Him for better, for worse, in all estates and conditions, with all His inconveniences as well as His privileges, with His poverty, His imprisonments, His reproaches, His deaths, His dangers, His conflicts, and the like. That is to say, you must choose Him with a willing resolution of mind to undergo all this as His call and for His sake. And this, indeed, is to close with Him in His own way and upon His own terms.

6. *Be sure that you choose Christ often, and think it not one single act or work only to choose and embrace Him.* If you would indeed make sure of Christ and an espousal to Him, you should choose and embrace Him anew every day. We are apt to look upon the work of choosing and embracing Christ as one single act or work that should be often repeated. By often repeating it, we should grow sound, more strong, more distinct in it. As a second edition corrects the errors of the first, so acts of believing, in this kind, supply the defects of the first act. Indeed, my advice to you is that you would make as much conscience of choosing and embracing Christ

every day as of praying every day, especially if you are
either young beginners in believing or old believers
under clouds and darkness. St. Paul made fresh
choices of Christ to the very last, Philippians 3:8-9. And
it is the duty of them that believe to believe: "These
things write I unto you," says St. John, "that believe on
the name of the Son of God, that ye may believe on the
name of the Son of God." They believed, and he would
have them to believe afresh every day. And so would I
have you do. Every day renew the first great act of faith
in your closing with Christ, and so shall every day be a
day of espousals between Christ and you. And so by
degrees shall you come to the sense and comfort of
this espousal. I have read of some who never came to a
sight and sense of their union with Christ till they took
this course.

Thus I have now shown you the way how you may
come to be espoused to Christ, as well as what a
Husband He is, what great things He does for His
spouses, and how much His heart is set upon an espousal with sinners. Now, will you take this course or
shall all be lost with you? Possibly the whole will have a
different effect upon those that read or hear these
things. Some, I hope, will be won and gained to Christ
by them. Others, I fear, will reject and despise all, and
that either out of a spirit of profaneness or insensibility
of their need of, or concernedness in, these things. If
any soul shall reject them out of a spirit of profaneness,
I would say to such a soul, as Solomon to the scorner,
Proverbs 9:12: "If thou scornest, thou alone shalt bear
it." You alone shall bear all your sins and all the wrath
and vengeance of God due to them. If any shall reject
these things out of a spirit of insensibility of their need

of and concern in them, their case is the more to be pitied. For the more insensible they are of their misery without Christ, the greater is that misery of theirs. "What is more miserable," says St. Augustine, "than for a miserable man not to commiserate Himself?" Others, it may be, stand doubting and trembling, daring neither to reject nor yet to embrace—not to reject because their need of Christ is so great, the worth of Christ so eminent, and the rejection of Christ so black, nor yet embrace because their sins are so many and their unworthiness so great. To such I would say, cease your trembling and delay your closing with Christ no longer. It has been your sin, let it be your shame and sorrow that you have refused and neglected Christ so long, saying with Augustine, "I have loved Thee too late, O Thou so ancient and yet so new a beauty. I have loved Thee too late."

And for your encouragement, I would say to you, as the servant did to his lord upon such an occasion as this, "Lord, it is done as you have commanded, and yet there is no room." Though many sinners, and great sinners, have been received to mercy, yet still there is room for you, and for all who have a mind for Christ. There is room in Christ's heart. There is room in Christ's arms. There is room in His covenant. There is room in His kingdom. There is room upon His throne with His Father for you. Therefore, as life and death are once more set before you, so I beseech you to choose life and not death that you may live forever.

Chapter 12

*Being a contemplation of the infinite love and condescension
of Christ to souls, and the unspeakable comfort and happiness
of believers in this sweet espousal*

In view of all that has been hitherto declared, we
may well take up an admiring contemplation of
Christ's love and condescension and the believer's
comfort and happiness—the one and the other being
exceeding great and glorious. O for Christ to marry
poor souls to Himself and for poor souls to be married
to Christ, how great is the love of the one and the happiness of the other herein!

1. *How great is the love and condescension of Christ in
marrying souls to Himself!* Next to His becoming man
and dying for them, wherein can He testify greater love
and condescension to them than in this? There are,
among many others that might be mentioned that will
argue His love and condescension herein to be wonderful and glorious, two things: one is the infinite disparity and disproportion between the parties, Him and
them, and the other is the unspeakable nearness and
gloriousness of that union and relation which He takes
them into with Himself, both of which I desire to contemplate.

1.) Contemplate the infinite disparity and disproportion between Him and them. What proportion
is there between a king and a beggar? What proportion

is there between an ant and an angel? Yea, between the
smallest worm and the angels in heaven? Infinitely less
proportion is there between Christ and sinners, and
yet He espouses them to Himself. What shall I say? He
is both high and great; we are base and vile. He is
blessed and glorious; we are wretched and despicable.
He is a great king; we are poor slaves and vassals, yea,
the worst of slaves and vassals, being the slaves and vassals of sin and Satan. And, to sum up all in a few words,
He is God and we are creatures; yea, He is an infinitely
pure and holy God and we are unspeakably impure
and unholy creatures. O how great is the disproportion! And yet He marries us to Himself.

What proportion is there between God and the
creature? The creature at best is but a small drop of being, but God is a sea, a fountain, an ocean of being.
The creature is and has but a little good, but God is a
most infinitely infinite good. The creature is a depen-
dent thing; the being of the creature is a depending
being; the very nature of the creature lies much in dependence. But God is an absolute and independent
being, He being of Himself and from Himself. Indeed,
all other things are "of Him and from Him and to
Him" as the Scripture speaks. Now, for God to marry
the creature and espouse the creature to Himself, O
what love, what condescension, is this! And, yet,
greater love than this does Christ show, for what
greater proportion is there between an infinitely holy
God and universally sinful, defiled, and polluted creatures? The distance between God and us as creatures is
great, but the distance between the infinitely holy God
and us as sinners is, in some sort, unspeakably greater.
It is our duty, and should be our joy, to know and keep

our creature distance with God. We should rejoice to
know that God is infinitely above us, but it is our misery. And we should tremble to think of our sinful distance from God, that distance, I mean, that sin is and
has caused between God and us.

2.) Contemplate the unspeakable nearness and
gloriousness of that union and relation which He takes
them into with Himself. As the distance and disproportion between the parties is infinitely great, so the union
and relation He takes them into is very near and glorious. The union between the vine and the branches is
near; the union and relation between the head and the
members is near; the union and relation between the
husband and wife is near. But all these are but shadows
and representations of that union and relation which
Christ takes believers into with Himself, which must,
therefore, be nearer and greater than all. It is, indeed
(as upon occasion has been before declared), next, for
intimacy and glory, to the essential and personal
union. Yea, it comes so near the highest union of all,
the union that is between the Father and the Son, as
that it is set forth in Scripture by the same expression
that that union is, namely, by "being and dwelling in
each other." Yea, Christ Himself seems to bring it so
near that great union that He makes that the pattern
of it, and accordingly He prays for it for His people:
"Neither pray I for these alone, but them also which
shall believe on Me through their word, that they all
may be one, as Thou, Father, art in Me, and I in Thee,
that they also may be one in us," John 17:21. Pray,
mark: He prays for the accomplishment of His union
for them as the top and perfection of all their happiness. And not only so, but as that which comes as near

the great union between His Father and Himself as can well be conceived. It is a sweet saying which one of the ancients has upon these words of Christ: "What more glorious than this union? What further or higher, poor soul, can you either have or desire to have than this: you shall be one with your bridegroom? O happy, exceeding happy, yea, of all others most happy, union!" In a word, nearer than this creatures cannot well be taken into Christ, nor can they have a greater glory put upon them in their being taken into this union and relation to Him. How great, therefore, must the love and condescension of Christ herein to believers be! O for Him to take such so near Himself as to make them one with Him, to lay them in His bosom, to communicate Himself to them; this is love indeed, and this we should contemplate and admire!

2. *How great is the comfort and happiness of believers in being thus married and espoused to Christ!* We say of such or such a woman that is well married, that she is well disposed of, and is very happy in, a husband. But, O soul, how well are you disposed of, who are disposed of to Christ? And how happy are you in a husband who are married to Him? What, soul, married to Jesus, to sweet Jesus, to lovely Jesus, to Jesus the Son of God! O what sweet, what strong consolation may this be to you! And how should it fill your heart with holy triumph and exultation forever! This alone may comfort you in all difficulties and troubles of life, and in all the conflicts and agonies of death. But yet to raise this comfort and happiness of yours a little higher, that you may rejoice in your lot, the lines being fallen to you in pleasant places, consider three things:

1.) Consider that this relation of yours to Christ
gives you full interest in Him and all that is His. Being
espoused to Christ, Christ is yours; and Christ being
yours, His blood is yours, His righteousness is yours,
His love is yours, His fullness is yours, the fruit of all
His sufferings, the virtue of all His offices, the sweetness of all His relations is yours. Christ being yours, all
is yours—all the promises are yours, all the ordinances
are yours, life is yours, death is yours, eternity is yours,
things present are yours, things to come are yours. O
what a goodly heritage have you, and how should your
soul bless the Lord that ever He drew you into this
union and relation to Him! What a spring of comfort
may this be to you in all conditions! "Fear not, for thou
shalt not be ashamed." Why? "For thy Maker is thy Husband," Isaiah 54:4-5. The truth is, though possibly you
may have little of this world, yet in having Christ you
have all you need and are capable of to make you
happy forever.

2.) Consider that this union and relation of
yours to Christ remains firm and steadfast forever. And
O what sweetness does this add unto it! "True," may
the soul say, "this relation is a blessed relation and full
of sweetness and comfort; but will it hold?" Yea, it will
hold, and that forever. The best comforts you have enjoyed here below will shortly have a period; and the
sweetest relations you stand in here will, after awhile,
be dissolved and broken. But your union and relation
to Christ will last forever. It can never be dissolved. "I
will betroth you unto Me," says God, "yea, I will betroth
you unto Me."

"But, Lord, for how long?" the soul may say.

"Why, forever," says God, Hosea 2:19. O that word,

"forever," as one observes upon this place, makes a misery (though but small in itself) an infinite misery, and a mercy (though but small in itself) even an infinite mercy. How much more does it make that which, in itself, is so great, as your union and espousal to Christ is, sweet and desirable!

"O but," says the soul, "never was there such a wretch as I am; never did any carry it towards Christ as I do. True, He has made love to me, and I have some hopes that I have closed with Him in a marriage covenant; but, alas! there never was such a rebellious, revolting, backsliding heart as mine. I am ever playing the harlot and going a-whoring from Him; by means of which, I fear, He will break union and communion with me, and at last cast me off."

I answer, truly, soul, this is very sad, and you should lie low under the sense of it. Yet, to encourage you against your fears, consider four things:

First, consider that Christ is not forward to take advantage against souls for their failing and breaking with Him. He is not strict to mark what is done amiss. He is not prone to cast off and to put away; no, it is what He hates, Malachi 2:16. True, He may, and many time does, withdraw from us and frown on us, but putting away He loves not. Yea, He pities and spares us under our infirmities, and His heart is moved for us.

Second, consider that, before ever Christ made love to you and took you into relation with Himself, He knew perfectly what manner of one you would be, and how you would carry it towards Him, and yet all could not hinder Him from showing this favor to you. Why, then, should you think it would cause Him to break with you now? The soul may be apt to say, "Did Christ think I would be such a wretch that I would carry it so unworthily towards Him under all His love as I do?" Yea, soul, Christ thought it, He knew it perfectly beforehand. In Deuteronomy 31:21 it is said that God knew what Israel would do beforehand. So Christ knew beforehand how you would slight His love, grieve His Spirit, and violate His laws. He knew how you would offend and affront Him by a proud, vain, wanton behavior before Him. He knew how you would backslide and go a-whoring from Him. And had He not seen and known that He had love enough to cover and pass by all, He would never have made love to you. Hence, when He betroths, He is said to do it in judgment. Christ knew what He did, and what a one He married, when He married you to Himself. And as all could not hinder His love at first, so neither shall it take off His love from you now.

Third, consider that you may have many failings and miscarriages, be guilty of many breakings with Christ and departures from Him, and yet the marriage covenant between Him and you is not broken. A woman may be guilty of many failings and miscarriages, and yet all not break the marriage covenant between her husband and her. And so it is here. O how sweet is that Scripture, Psalm 89:30-34, "If his children forsake My law, and walk not in My judgments; if they break My statutes, and keep not My commandments; then will I visit their transgressions with a rod, and their iniquity with stripes." And what follows? "Nevertheless My lovingkindness will I not utterly take from him, nor suffer My faithfulness to fail. My covenant will I not break, nor alter the thing that is gone out of My lips." Pray mark, Christ's people may sin, and sin greatly, and He may chastise them for their sins. Yea, He may seem to take away His lovingkindness from them, and may, for a time, really suspend the influences and manifestations thereof. But His covenant love and faithfulness to them remains firm and steadfast to them forever, notwithstanding all. So again, Jeremiah 3:1 and 14, "Thou hast played the harlot with many lovers, yet return again to me, saith the Lord. Turn, O backsliding children, for I am married unto you." Mark, though they had backslidden, though they had played the harlot with many lovers, yet Christ owns His covenant relation to them, and with them. Yea, and He sends, as it were, His covenant after them and by that fetches them home to Himself. O whatever your miscarriages are, whatever your breakings with Christ and departures from Him, yet, being once married to Him, the marriage union and relation between Him and you remains firm and steadfast forever, notwithstanding all.

Fourth, consider that it is not long ere the Lord Jesus, your dear Husband, will consummate the marriage between Him and your soul. And O how sweet will this be! The match here is, at it were, begun between Christ and you, but Christ will shortly come and consummate it. "Behold, the bridegroom cometh"; and again, "They that were ready went into the marriage; and the Marriage of the Lamb is come." There is a time when Christ will come to consummate the marriage between Him and souls. When He comes as to the world, He comes as a judge to condemn it, to avenge the quarrel of His covenant, the quarrel of His blood, all which they have rejected. He comes to pass sentence upon them for resisting His Spirit, for condemning his grace, for breaking His laws, for neglecting His salvation. And O how dark will the day of His coming be to them! But not to His own spouses—when He comes He comes as a Bridegroom. And O how sweet will this coming of His be to them!

Then Christ will solemnly present you to His Father as His spouse in the presence of all His holy angels. And O how joyful and glorious will this be! In Genesis 24:67 we read that Isaac took Rebekah and brought her into his mother's tent. So, when dear Jesus comes to consummate the marriage between Him and you, He will, being attended with all His holy angels, bring you into His Father's house and will there present you to Him as His spouse, saying, "Father, here is My spouse. Here is one whom in the day of everlasting love Thou gavest unto Me, one whom I have redeemed to Myself by My blood, and married to Myself by My Spirit in the gospel. This is he who I was made sin and a curse for, and though he was in his blood and gore when I first made love to him, yet lo! now here he is spotless and faultless before Thee. Father, own him as Thy Son's spouse, and delight in him forever."

O how sweet, how glorious, will this be! Suppose some great prince were married, and, upon his marriage, should take his spouse in his hand and lead her into the presence chamber of the king, his father, and there present her to him to the end he might take notice of her as his son's spouse and show suitable respect and favor to her. What a sweet thing would this be! But alas, what is this to the presentation Christ will make of you to His Father at His coming, who will then "present thee faultless into the presence of His glory with exceeding joy," Jude 24! When David and the elders of Israel brought up the ark from the house of Obed Edom, it was with great joy and shouting. But O when Christ, attended with all His holy angels, shall bring and present you into the presence of His Father, what joy and shoutings will there then be! Surely there will be great rejoicing on all hands. God the Father will greatly rejoice. Christ the Son will greatly rejoice. God the Holy Ghost will greatly rejoice. The angels will greatly rejoice. Your soul also will greatly rejoice. God the Father will greatly rejoice to see His Son's spouse come home to Him so richly decked and adorned; Christ the Son will greatly rejoice that He has gotten His spouse into His arms and bosom, never to part with her again. The Holy Ghost will greatly rejoice to see His work in tying the marriage knot between Christ and the soul completed. The angels will greatly rejoice as being friends both to the Bridegroom and bride, and as partaking with them in the marriage supper. And you yourself will greatly rejoice in that now your happiness is consummated, and you shall forever lie in the bosom and embraces of your Husband's love. O how sweet, how glorious will this be!

3. *Then Christ will lead you into the bride chamber, the mansion He has prepared for you in the Father's house where you shalt dwell forever in His presence and sit down eternally with Him at the marriage feast.* And O how sweet and glorious will this be! Being thus beautified and presented to the Father, what now remains for you but to enter upon your lot with all the saints, and to possess the jointure Christ made you in the time of your espousal to Him, even eternal life and glory with Himself forever! What now remains for you but to sit down in the

full views of His glory, the full visions of His face, the full enjoyment of His presence, the full embraces of His bosom, the full incomes of His love, and all forever? Here in the day of espousal, you have had some views of Him. You have seen His back parts, but then you shall behold His glory forever. Here you have seen Him through a glass darkly, but then you shall see Him face to face. Your visions of Him shall be both full and immediate. Here there have been some intercourses of love and delight kept up between Him and you. You have had some of the kisses of His mouth, some embraces in His bosom, but then you shall have your fill of His love, being sweetly immersed and swallowed up in the ocean of it forever. O how sweet will this be! When Christ and your soul have met in an ordinance, how often have you said with Peter, "It is good to be here." And, when He has given you, now and then, a little taste of His love, how have you been ravished with it, crying out with the spouse, "Thy love is better than wine!" But O what will it be to enjoy all this in its fullness, and that without the least moment's interruption forever! When Christ and your soul shall meet, not in a duty and ordinance only but in heaven, in the Father's house, all you have here of Him is but now and then a kiss of His mouth, now and then a taste, a visit, a descent of His grace and love; yet this is sweet, and makes a little heaven in your soul. But when He comes to consummate the marriage, then you shall have everlasting embraces and uninterrupted pourings out of love from Him. Then no more veilings of His face, no more withdrawings of His presence, no more suspensions of His love from you, but you shall sit down in the full enjoyment of all forever.

"But," may some doubting soul say, "true, here is comfort and happiness enough for all Christ's spouses; and were I assured of my espousal to Him I should think it enough to carry me through both life and death with comfort. But I am afraid I have neither part nor lot in this matter."

I answer, if you are one who loves your sins and lives in them, if you are one who allows and indulges yourself in your lusts, yea, in any known lust or sin, be it small or great, then you have great ground for such fears. For I must tell you that the spouses of Christ are of another disposition. They hate sin and love holiness, and do what in them lies to flee the one and pursue after the other. But I will at present look upon you to be a poor doubting spouse of Christ who makes this complaint, and so shall take a double word of encouragement with you as to this, and thereby put a conclusion to this matter:

1.) I would speak to you as Samuel sometimes did to Saul in another case, namely when Saul told him that he had performed the commandment of the Lord. "If so," says Samuel, "what then means this bleating of the sheep in mine ears, and the lowing of the oxen which I hear?" So, if you have indeed no part nor lot in Christ, then what do the bleedings, mournings, and lamentings of your soul mean under the sense of your distance and estrangement from Christ, and your utter unsuitableness to Him both in spirit and life? "Blessed are they that mourn, for they shall be comforted," Matthew 5:3. What do your high valuations of Him and the vehement hungerings and thirstings of your soul after Him mean? "Blessed are they that hunger and thirst after righteousness, for they shall be

satisfied," Matthew 5:6. What do the holy tremblings of
the soul in the thoughts of sinning against Him, your
care and solicitude to please Him, your fear to offend
Him, mean? It is the character of a loyal wife that her
care is to please her husband and not to offend him.
What do your sensibleness of, and mournings under,
the dishonors of Christ with the longing of your soul
after His exaltation mean? "The reproaches of them
that reproach him do fall on thee," Psalm 69:9. It is the
spirit of a loyal spouse to be concerned for her husband's concernments. These and many more such gracious dispositions as are found in you speak comfortably in your soul in this case—though still I would have
you press after the clearest evidences, and the fullest
assurance of your espousal to Him.

2.) Suppose the worst; yet, for your encouragement, I would speak to you as the disciples to the blind
man, Mark 10:49: "Be of good comfort, arise, Christ
calleth thee." He calls you into these blessed espousals
with Himself. And you that would do as that blind man
there did, who arose and came to Jesus, assure yourself
of this: His arms are wide open to receive you. Truly,
whoever or whatever you are that makes this complaint, whether spouse or no spouse, your proper and
immediate work is now to close with Christ in a marriage covenant. For pray, mark: The work of a convinced sinner and of a doubting, beclouded saint is the
same here. The one as well as the other is to believe
and close with Christ, as if he had never done it before.

Thus have I now done, saint, spouse of Christ. What
remains but that you love, reverence, and obey your
Lord and Head, living a life of dependence upon Him,
as also of longing expectation of His coming to con-

summate the marriage between Him and you? What remains but that you should take up the words of the Apostle, making the same inference from your espousal to Christ that he does from the dissolution of all things, saying in his own name and others, "What manner of persons ought we to be, in all manner of conversation and godliness, looking for, and hastening the coming of the day of God!"

Sinner, what remains for you to do but to give up your name and soul to Christ in a marriage covenant and be happy forever? I will conclude all with those words, Revelation 19:9, "Blessed are they which are called to the marriage supper of the Lamb."

Soli Deo Gloria